The de Némethy Method

Bertalan de Némethy on Adam II in Munich, Germany, 1939.

The de Némethy Method

MODERN TECHNIQUES FOR
TRAINING THE SHOW JUMPER
AND ITS RIDER

Bertalan de Némethy

Instructional Photographs by Alix Coleman
Drawings by Heather St. Clair Davis

Doubleday
NEW YORK   LONDON   TORONTO   SYDNEY   AUCKLAND

To my darling wife
EMILY

without whose enthusiasm, encouragement, and dedication
this book would never have been completed.

Published by Doubleday, a division of
Bantam Doubleday Dell Publishing Group, Inc.,
666 Fith Avenue, New York, New York 10103

Doubleday and the portrayal of an anchor with a dolphin
are trademarks of Doubleday, a division of
Bantam Doubleday Dell Publishing Group, Inc.

Published in the UK in 1990 by Partridge Press
A division of Transworld Publishers Ltd
61/63 Uxbridge Road, London W5 5SA

A CIP catalogue record for this book is available from the British Library

Library of Congress Cataloging-in-Publication Data
De Némethy, Bertalan.
    The de Némethy method.
    Includes index.
    1. Horsemanship.   I. Title.
SF309.D255   1988   799.2   87-13688
ISBN 0-385-23620-4

BUCKINGHAM PALACE.

Any number of riders have had great success in one or other of the equestrian sports, but once in a very long while a true genius emerges who seems to have an instinctive comprehension of the relationship between horse and rider. Bertalan de Nemethy has shown exactly how to achieve the very best performance from this relationship. No-one need look any further than this book for confirmation of that statement.

I never got beyond the first steps in show jumping, but during many years as President of the International Equestrian Federation I was able to appreciate his genius as a trainer and as an original thinker and course designer. I am quite sure that many generations of competitors will be grateful to him for giving them the benefit of his views and ideas in this invaluable book.

1989

Foreword

Though innumerable instructional books are published every year, it remains highly unusual to find one such as this. To begin with, it is based entirely on the author's personal experience, which is not always the case. Next, he wrote it all himself, which is even rarer. And best of all, he has much to say that is distinctly original, having himself devised key elements of the system he elaborates on the following pages.

Born in Hungary, Bertalan de Némethy had decided by the age of ten that he wanted to devote his life to horses. Early competitive successes as a fencer and modern pentathlete failed to divert this ambition, and in due course he entered the Royal Hungarian Military Academy. Soon after graduation he was appointed to the Military Riding Instructor School, from which he emerged as that institution's youngest instructor as well as a member of his nation's jumping team for the ill-fated 1940 Olympic Games. In these roles he competed extensively in Europe and was selected to study and observe at the German Cavalry School, and he very likely would have remained a career officer in Hungary had not the cataclysm of World War II intervened. This accident of fate and history not only exposed him to a far wider variety of equestrian experiences than he probably would have encountered as a cavalry officer (which may well have proven synergistic), but also brought him eventually to our shores. Thus it was the U.S. Equestrian Team that became the prime beneficiary of de Némethy's single-minded devotion to the systematic development of the jumping horse, and his genius as a trainer, teacher, and course-designer.

The contents of de Némethy's book speak for themselves, and the half century of practical experience that went into them. They have proven their value countless times during his twenty-five-year tenure as coach of the USET jumping squad, and subsequently, too—all at the very highest levels of equestrian sport, in World Cup, World Championship, and Olympic competition. It should be noted that de Némethy also verified from the horse's back the techniques he recommends; every single USET horse pictured in this book benefited from his own riding, as well as from his coaching from the ground.

When one considers the influence de Némethy's teaching has had, not only through his own riders and their pupils in turn, but also through those in other countries who have been influenced by their examples, it is hard to overestimate its importance. Many observers today regard the American showjumping style as both the most attractive and the most effective of any, and results seem to bear them out. There are, of course, many reasons for this happy state of affairs, but if I had to name the single individual who has made the greatest contribution to it since World War II, my vote would go to "Bert."

Despite this very far-reaching influence, relatively few riders have been privileged to study with de Némethy personally, and even these lucky few have never possessed his ideas in writing. Thus horsemen everywhere must be grateful to him for the pains he has taken (he would not dispute that choice of words) to record his ideas in print and picture in an organized, logical progression that can be read, reread, and pondered. I am confident that it will prove a valued legacy for generations of riders to come.

WILLIAM STEINKRAUS
OLYMPIC CHAMPION, 1968
CHAIRMAN OF THE BOARD,
U.S. EQUESTRIAN TEAM

Acknowledgments

My grateful appreciation to my dear former assistant, Ellen Raidt Lordi, for her superior demonstrations for the instructional photographs; to her husband, Peter Francis Lordi, for his generosity in providing the horses; and to Jacqueline Kennedy Onassis for her generous interest and support.

Author's Note

There are several arbitrary editorial treatments in this book to which the reader's attention should be called. First, the author knows that horses and riders may be of either sex; nonetheless, for clarity, I have chosen to refer to the rider as "he" and the horse as "it" throughout, and hope that readers will take no offense. Secondly, it is perhaps more correct to call the littlest form of jump a "cavalletto" in its singular form, and "cavalletti" only in the plural, following the Italian word from which the term has come to us; in this case, I have chosen to follow the latest Webster's, which prefers "cavalletti" for both the singular and plural. The somewhat old-fashioned "longe" has been preferred to "lunge" as an equestrian term, as being both more correct and more traditional. And finally, in referring to obstacles in the main text, only feet and inches have been used for heights and distances, in the confidence that those who "think metric" will readily translate. Both sets of figures have been provided in the Appendix.

The photographs of former United States Equestrian Team members over fences have been selected to show the consistency of style of both the horses and the riders. All the horses in the photographs were trained at the USET headquarters, using the methods described in the following pages.

The historic photographs of the author at various international shows demonstrate the results of applying the training methods explained in the text.

Contents

Introduction

An Historical Overview
of Horses and Horsemanship

We humans have a natural, inborn curiosity about the past and the unknown world: space, the origin and evolution of the earth, the depth of the oceans, and the life and purpose of our ancestors. Such curiosity also stimulates our interest in the fascinating world of animals, making us want to discover their origins, follow their evolution, explore their way of life, their nature and development, and study their struggle for survival.

While the evolution of mankind is closely related to that of animals, it would be naive or even hypocritical to speak of a great traditional friendship between us. The fact is that, for various reasons, we have actually exploited most of them—including the horse. Before discovering their value for higher purposes, we even hunted and killed horses as a source of food and clothing.

Although the very first relationship between man and horse was one of predator and prey, somewhere in ancient Asia or Europe man acquired the idea of capturing the horse alive. Even today researchers disagree as to the first utilization of the horse, but it seems most logical to presume that it was used to haul things before it was mounted. Most likely, horse power was first used in farming, thereby making life much easier for our ancestors. Later, traveling longer distances for exploration was the motivation for using horses as a means of transportation, which thus enabled man to achieve his ambitions of power, wealth, and independence. It is widely believed that the Chinese, Persians, and Greeks began to use the horse as a beast of burden and transportation, soldiers initially riding bareback on their way to combat.

Use of the horse's speed came only later, after the saddle and stirrup had been invented. Prior to the tenth century B.C., the Chinese mounted horses for purposes of hunting, parade, and war. And archeologists have discovered much evidence attesting to the use of the horse in pulling four-wheeled vehicles, thus elevating this animal to an instrument of power and authority.

Throughout the centuries Egyptians, Chinese, and Persians increasingly applied the horse's skills to military tactics, fashioning a war machine capable of speed—and therefore of surprise attack. Due to its successful collaboration in warfare, the horse was ever more glorified.

From the steppes of Eurasia through Mongolia, nomads on horseback arrived in Central Europe, further travel prevented only by the desert near the river Tisza (in Alfold, modern Hungary). The Tartar invasion, starting in eastern Mongolia and confined to Europe, was based on the use of hundreds of thousands of Mongolian horses, led by the genius Genghis Khan (1260–95). Astride his war steed, Khan conquered China, crushed the Turks in Central Asia, and advanced as far as the Adriatic Sea. It is fascinating to study the histories, migrations, and conquests of the ancient invaders, and their masterful use of cavalry power. Their victories were due to well-trained, fast horses who could change direction extremely rapidly while their riders, braced standing in the stirrups, shot bows and arrows.

As time passed, growing regard for the horse as man's servant and collaborator developed into reverence, and then almost into a cult. In the Middle Ages, complicated maneuvering of the horse demanded more sophisticated handling. Equitation, as such, improved considerably since medieval tournaments required an improved and safer seat for the rider, and greater control of the horse. The emergence of the Renaissance ushered in an even more advanced era of equitation.

Such, in brief, was the evolution of the horse from a source of food, to war machine, to its present elevated status as a creature of great beauty, whose possession and utilization are regarded as the epitome of sport, entertainment, and luxury.

Having briefly reviewed the evolution of the horse, let us now turn to the literature dealing with horses that has grown up throughout the centuries. Let me emphasize that, in order to participate seriously in any sport or artistic endeavor, a sound technique must be learned and applied if one is to achieve successful results; blind practice alone is insufficient. If we are to master the whats, whys, and hows of riding and training a horse, we need to read and ponder the lessons of the past, to gain a solid understanding of the theories and principles embodied in established equestrian literature. No one should underestimate the value of such theoretical knowledge.

Thus, while it is not my goal to discuss the hundreds of books that have been written on horsemanship, I would be remiss if I failed to mention the teachings of some of the great masters of earlier times.

The first of all was Simon of Athens, a professional riding master of the fourth century B.C. While only fragments of his teachings have survived, he exerted a tremendous influence upon Xenophon (430–354 B.C.), a Greek historian, soldier, statesman, and horseman, whose authoritative, practical

Bertalan de Némethy on Adam II in Vienna, Austria, 1939.

writings have been translated into English as well as many other languages. In *The Art of Horsemanship* (*Peri Hippike*), Xenophon quotes Simon of Athens many times, as he does again in his other masterpiece, *Commander of the Horse* (*Hipparchikos*). Xenophon's books represent the first organized writings on riding as an art. They reveal his profound understanding of the fundamental equestrian principles, as well as those of hippology and the handling, training, and care of horses. In an easy, uncomplicated style, he provides a fascinating study of the horsemanship of his time. Considering that Xenophon wrote nearly 2300 years ago, the fact that the validity of his principles endures today is ample evidence of his mastery.

While the use of horses for various purposes obviously continued during the Dark Ages, no further literature on riding has come down to us until that of the early Renaissance. The first printed book of that period to deal with equitation was *Gli Ordini di Cavalcare* (*Riding Rules*) by the Italian Federico Grisone, published in 1550, which merits attention if only because Grisone was familiar with airs above the ground and other relatively sophisticated movements. However, his training methods were often harsh, and today would not be considered acceptable. His most famous pupil, Pignatelli, opened the first great riding academy in Naples, where he trained Antoine de Pluvinel (1555–1620), who later became the riding master of Louis XIII of France. Pluvinel played an important role in the development of horsemanship as we know it today, being far superior to and more refined than any of his predecessors.

The next great riding master was an Englishman, the Duke of Newcastle (1592–1676), who described his original methods of training in his book *A General System of Horsemanship* (first published in a French translation in 1658). Newcastle exerted considerable influence upon his successors, including the great French master François Robichon de la Guérinière, who systematized all of the basic classic principles in his *École de Cavalerie* (1733). Among later writers the most outstanding is perhaps Gustav Steinbrecht (1858–1937), author of *Der Gymnasium des Pferdes* (probably the best book ever written on horsemanship).

It is difficult to obtain, much less read, all of the great books of the distant past; but luckily, valuable contemporary books are readily available. One of the most comprehensive is Waldemar Seunig's *Horsemanship* (1956), a classic in the field, which provides detailed explanations of many of the finer points involved in training the horse and rider. Lieutenant Colonel A. L. d'Endrödy's *Give Your Horse a Chance* (1959) is also a must for any serious rider. The correct answer to almost every equestrian question can be found in at least one of the above books. Both Colonel Seunig and Colonel d'Endrödy were not only skilled analysts and theoreticians, but also highly successful international competitors, and fine teachers.

In every human endeavor, certain lucky people are born more gifted than others; they succeed in competition faster and to a higher degree. This is usually attributed only to innate natural talent and instinct. But even such exceptional individuals need systematic guidance and instruction. The majority, of course, have even greater need of proven systems to follow, since such guidance helps compensate for lack of natural instinct, and provides the vicarious knowledge and experience necessary to ensure satisfactory progress.

I prefer not to call riding a science, as some have referred to it; rather, I consider it to be a sport, an athletic activity which in the hands of the most talented individuals can be upgraded to a fine art. The equestrian sport cannot be compared to any other, for it involves not only the physical abilities of the riders and their knowledge of equestrian theory, but also a true understanding of the relationship between man and animal. Most important, it requires proficiency in finding a medium for communication which can win the animal's confidence, thus avoiding the confusion and misunderstanding that invariably result in unhappiness or resistance. Since we can never hope to dominate the horse through force or muscular strength alone, it is obvious that we also need a genuine empathy for the horse (without demonstrating weakness), and a healthy dose of common sense, to ensure final success.

(Opposite top) Bertalan de Némethy on Adam II in Rome, Italy, 1940.
(Bottom) Bertalan de Némethy on Adam II in Aachen, Germany, 1939.

Bertalan de Némethy on Duce over a water jump in Lucerne, Switzerland, 1938.

1. Basic Principles of Equitation

The vast majority of my equestrian career has been involved with the training and development of jumping horses and their riders; it is these subjects that make up the heart of this book. Readers may thus be surprised to find that I have not commenced by dealing immediately with jumping techniques, but rather with topics that may seem far removed from them.

From my experience in giving clinics, I am well aware that many riders find discussions of the basic principles of equitation and the physiology of the horse boring, and they can't wait to build the fences and start attacking them. My experience is, however, that when they never achieve a clear understanding of the basic principles, they never learn to ride really well, no matter how great their natural talent. For nothing of any substance can be built on a flimsy foundation, and the horse and the rider who don't know what they are doing will always fall far short of realizing their full potential. That is why this book starts with a discussion of basic fundamentals.

What, then, are the basic principles that govern the riding and training of the jumper? They are to be found on the flat, not at the jump itself. I think that the base considerations are four in number; they are concerned with straightness, crookedness, calmness, and forwardness. I will deal with them in that order, and then discuss the related ideas of balance and rhythm.

Gustav Steinbrecht, who is still regarded by many as the greatest German master of equestrian art, offered a simple summation of the basic principles of riding: "Ride your horse forward, and keep it straight." The famous French general L'Hotte agreed, but found it necessary to rank calmness even ahead of the other concepts; his own motto was "calm, forward and straight."

These principles, being based on the lifelong experience of two great riding masters, deserve to be considered in detail, and scrutinized in the cold light of common sense. For example, we must ask ourselves whether it is right for us to concentrate first on relentless obedience to forward movement, or should we first make the horse's position straight?

We must remember that the two concepts, *riding forward* and *making the horse straight,* are in fact interrelated. In other words, the horse will resist the demand for forward obedience if it is not straight within its body position, for, if it is crooked, the harmonious, flowing forward movement will be disturbed. Indeed, resistance usually originates due either to crookedness, or mental or temperamental difficulties. On the other hand, keeping the body straight in the absence of any willingness to move forward is hardly possible. Consequently, before deciding which of the two basic principles should receive priority, we must consider their basic definitions and analyze the feelings linked to them.

Straightness

When is the horse straight in its body position? The first answer must be, "When the entire length of its spinal column describes a straight line, with no longitudinal deviation whatsoever." This is easy to verify when the horse is at a standstill; the hind legs are in line with the forelegs, and it appears, when one stands on the ground, that the entire weight of the body is evenly distributed throughout (though in reality it is not).

When the horse is mounted or starts to move, its physical situation changes. While in movement, its spine shows some lateral deviation from the straight position, with some flexion in the ribs resulting from various sequences of different gaits. Otherwise, when the hind legs follow the forelegs in the direction of motion, the horse is straight. We can confirm this by looking at the horse as it moves toward us; the forelegs almost hide the hind legs, but because the horse is narrower between its shoulders than between its hips, we can see the outside lines of the hind legs behind the forelegs.

Ultimately, our perspective from the saddle affords the easiest method of recognizing the horse's straightness. When one sits evenly on both seat bones, keeping one's hipbones naturally straight above them, the lower legs remain in the same position on both sides. We can feel and see the horse's shoulders moving evenly and parallel to each other. Its neck is straight, and directly in front of the middle of our body. Its ears are even, and we can barely see its eyebrows. Our contact with its mouth is the same on both sides. In conclusion, when all these factors exist, the horse is straight in its body position.

The straightness of the horse's body can in most cases be stabilized and improved upon through systematic elementary training: lateral and longitudinal bendings, flexion exercises, leg-yieldings, shoulder-ins, shoulder-outs, turns, turns on the haunches, turns on the forehand, half-passes, traverses, reins-back, and many transitions. Each one of these elementary training movements will be discussed in greater detail later in this book.

Straightness as viewed from the front: The horse is straight in its body. The forelegs are covering the hind legs. The horse's neck and head are perfectly in the center of the rider's upper body. Very correct.

Straightness as viewed from behind: The hind legs cover the forelegs. The rider's upper body is perfectly straight.

Crookedness as viewed from the front: The right hind leg moves between the forelegs.

Crookedness as viewed from behind: The horse's left hind leg has pushed the rider's seat to the right. The left foreleg shows up between the hind legs.

Crookedness

The opposite of straightness is crookedness. When is the horse crooked in its body position? If the horse is in motion, and we are looking at ground level from in front or from behind, it is when one of its hind legs deviates from the direction of the motion, and moves outside of the foreleg's line. The other hind leg moves in the direction of the middle of its body, in between the forelegs. In more severe crookedness, the whole body of the horse is curved, with the hindquarters being completely out of line.

What feeling do we get when we are sitting on a horse that is crooked in its body? If one of the hind legs deviates, we should immediately feel it through our seat. The deviating hind leg pushes and transfers more weight to the opposite shoulder and, accordingly, pushes our seat to that side. The horse's neck bends in the direction of the deviating hind leg, and the body becomes hollow—or bent—to a certain degree on that side. The horse tries to find support in our opposite hand by stiffening its jaw and, if it can find that support, by adding weight to it. On the opposite side, the ribs are curved outwardly, indicating that our leg is not accepted and, indeed, is being thrown away. In essence, the whole direction of the movement inclines toward the side to which weight was transferred by the deviating hind leg.

At this point, a few differing opinions regarding the sources of crookedness should be mentioned. One, regarded by many as a fact, is that no horse is ever absolutely straight, just as no human body is ever perfectly bilaterally developed. Every horse has a hollow side and a stiff side (which is usually the left side). Crookedness can also be attributed to faulty conformation or physical asymmetry.

Of course, some foals may even be born straight—and stay so until human hands touch them. For we as riders cannot escape the possibility that, by our own right- or left-handedness, lack of experience, faulty seat, or other influence, we may also contribute to the horse's crookedness.

Calmness

As we have noted, General L'Hotte ranked calmness before both straightness and forward obedience in summarizing his basic principles.

I hesitate to rank calmness equally with straightness and forwardness as a basic principle, since I feel that calmness is partly an innate trait of the horse's personality and temperament, and cannot always be learned, even through the most systematic training. Nervousness is often part of the individual horse's innate disposition, though it may also result from excessive physical training at too early an age, or improperly applied training methods. Whatever the cause, a diagnosis must be made. Sometimes we can partially alleviate nervousness with patience, knowledge, and experience, and if the cause is physical, we can obtain veterinary help. But often (with human beings as well as animals) a bad disposition, whether inherited or caused by unfortunate circumstances, can be difficult or impossible to change.

Calmness should not, of course, be confused with laziness or lack of interest. I regard calmness as the horse's pleasant and willing acceptance of its relationship with the rider, without resisting his domination and influence. A happy cooperation should exist between rider and horse, yet without the horse having to sacrifice its alertness, personality, or interest.

Forwardness

Few truly understand the equestrian meaning of the term "forwardness." For riding forward does not mean simply going forward in a relatively straight line. In equestrian terms, it means much more than that. The horse can go forward in some direction or other, in response to its rider's aids, but still lack forward obedience.

Nor does riding forward mean a horse that is in danger of running away, so that the rider loses complete control of its speed or regularity. Forward obedience means a calm willingness to accept the rider's signal to increase forward motion.

Liveliness and impulsion are both components of forward obedience, and neither should ever be confused with mere nervousness, the criterion being that the horse's regularity of movement must remain undisturbed. However, liveliness cannot be separated from impulsion, the latter being partly natural and a result of innate temperament, and partly something that is developed through proper training.

If this discussion of forward obedience still remains unclear to the reader, let me compare the horse that lacks forward obedience to an automobile that moves sluggishly because the driver presses the accelerator without having fully released the emergency brake.

To summarize, the horse which is ridden forward should remain relaxed, keen and happy, its rider confident in the knowledge that his influence is accepted just as he wishes it to be.

The horse's forward obedience will also be improved through systematic elementary training movements, especially the tactful application of leg communication coupled with careful and proper use of the whip, spurs, and lots of rewards. Riding cross-country at a trot, and canter on long, straight lines, uphill and downhill, are also indispensably helpful.

Having established the interrelationships among these four basic fundamentals of riding, we can now move on to two somewhat more complex concepts, without which the fundamentals could not accomplish the desired results. They are comparable in importance to the other basic principles, and must be equally well understood.

Maintaining the Horse's Natural Balance

All the classics of equestrian literature stress the importance of balance, and it is unquestionably an essential part of teaching and practice. Balance is defined, according to the laws of nature, as the equal distribution of weight around a center, making for a stabilized equilibrium. Balance is so important a part of riding that it is essential for us to clearly understand it.

Balance occurs in nature, existing in all living and nonliving matter. In living creatures balance is instinctive. Shifts of balance occur constantly but, though imbalances often occur, it is usually possible to regain complete balance instinctively. In addition to this inherent balance in nature, however, we must clearly recognize the special interpretation of equestrian balance.

Our own weight and position, as well as our systematic training of the horse to make it more comfortable for our purposes, interfere somewhat with the horse's natural balance. Though normally the weight of a skilled rider does not imbalance the horse to any considerable degree, a clumsy rider can interfere with it severely. We know how quickly we can reestablish our own balance after making a bad step, and how quickly a riderless horse can recover if it happens to slip into an extremely imbalanced position. However, if the rider inhibits the horse's mechanism of using its head and neck in order to regain balance, regaining it can be very difficult or even impossible.

A mild shift of balance is not disturbing; it happens naturally during any change of movement or position, and the horse simply adapts to its changed situation by adjusting its head and neck appropriately.

This brings us to the next important factor. What is really critical, and must always be taken into consideration, is the *center of gravity* of the horse, and its relationship to the rider's weight and position, combined with all movement and speed. The balance and center of gravity are permanently related.

Where is the *center of gravity* of the horse? This question can be answered in several ways. First, it is at the level of the sixth rib, just behind the point of the elbow and about two thirds of the way down from the top line along its back. Alternatively, if one makes a vertical line from behind the withers, and a horizontal line from the shoulder point to the buttock,

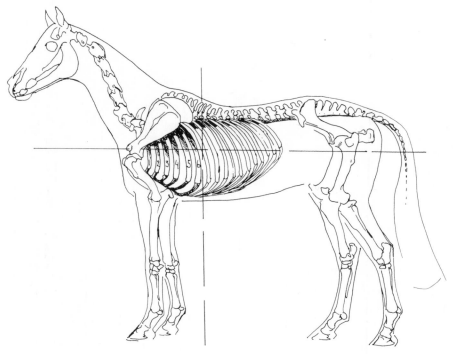

The horse's center of gravity in relation to its skeleton.

the point at which these two imaginary lines cross each other in the body of the horse would also be the center of gravity.

In practice, of course, the position of the horse's neck and head plays an important role in determining its center of gravity, for either raising or lowering the neck will alter the horse's weight distribution and thus move its center of gravity either forward or backward.

Maintaining the horse's natural balance is of primary importance in riding. This in turn depends upon the rider's ability to bring his own center of gravity into synchrony with that of the horse. The rider's position, as well as his weight, must be adjusted to the horse's movements; usually by the rider placing his body directly above or ahead of the horse's center of gravity, depending upon the horse's velocity.

The *center of gravity line* of the horse extends vertically through its center of gravity and moves in concert with it. Each lateral flexion shifts, to a certain degree, the center of gravity inside or outside in a similar way; as the horse's speed increases, the rider's center of gravity must be moved ahead of the horse's center of gravity line, while still maintaining an harmonious relationship. This theory clearly justifies the jockey's position in the race: close to the neck of the horse, ahead of its center of gravity. On the other hand, however, the dressage rider employs the opposite position

Kathy Kusner on Untouchable in Hickstead, England, 1968.

Kathy Kusner on Aberali in Aachen, Germany, 1967.

Kathy Kusner on Fleet Apple in the Munich Olympics, 1972.

while executing pirouettes or certain high school figures above the ground. In short, the rider must incline his upper body forward during all forward movement except for the free walk, but never so much that his center of gravity extends beyond the supporting area of the horse. (If that were to happen, the horse would have to move faster and faster in order to support its body, with the forehand attempting to maintain its natural equilibrium.)

The horse's natural balance can be maintained only if its weight is evenly distributed between its right and left pairs of legs, as well as between the forelegs and hind legs. When the horse's hindquarters are more engaged by the rider's influence, and its hind legs reach closer to the center of gravity line under its body, its hindquarters will sink, its center of gravity will move back, and its forehand will thus become somewhat relieved of carrying the added weight. Consequently, the horse will not need to accelerate, since less weight will be supported by its forehand and its natural balance can be preserved.

When this is achieved, we have found the equestrian balance Richard Wätjen had in mind when he wrote in his *Dressage Riding* that "Balance is the result of impulsion in harmony with collection."

These pictures beautifully demonstrate the rider's position and its relationship to the balance and center of gravity of the horse. In every picture, the rider is in complete harmony with the horse, maintaining perfect contact with its mouth. The rider's upper body is always in the right place, but her legs could be closer to the girth.

No two people are born with the same ability or feeling for coordinating with the horse's natural balance. Some people have a more refined feeling for balance than others, and thus have a special talent for riding. Similarly, certain horses tolerate interference from the rider better than others, and can accommodate themselves to an awkward rider more readily. Usually, it is the better bred horses that tend to be most sensitive in this regard; if their natural balance is disturbed continuously, they become confused, frightened, and discouraged, finally refusing to cooperate with the rider altogether.

Stabilizing the Horse's Rhythm

Balance and rhythm are equally essential to riding. The word rhythm, as applied to music and dance, generally connotes regularity. In our equestrian language, however, we take this idea a step further, and describe equestrian rhythm in terms of regulated impulsion, rhythmical motion, and forwardness.

Cadence is often confused with rhythm, for the terms are closely related; but there is still a subtle shade of difference between the two. The rhythmical movement of the horse is individualized, and depends upon the particular horse's conformation, size, and disposition. The horse's cadence, on the other hand, can be developed only in a more collected frame: the strides become shorter, the leg action becomes more elevated, and the sequence of the movements becomes slower. Since no horse will remain in its ideal rhythm at any gait instinctively, the rider must use his influence to discover and regulate it. When the rider is finally able to maintain this ideal natural rhythm, the horse's maximum stability is achieved.

2. The Physical Horse and Its Gaits

Before we get into the business of actually riding and communicating with the horse, I think it is important for the rider to have a clear understanding of the animal itself and how it functions. I would like to accomplish this by starting with a brief discussion of the horse's skeletal structure, then its senses and aptitudes, and finally its basic gaits and their variations.

The Physiological Structure of the Horse

Let us start with the structure of the front legs. It is obvious that the bone of the shoulder *(scapula)* and the bone of the arm *(humerus)* form an angle—the *scapula-humeral* angle; and that the *humerus* and the *radius* (forearm) form another angle; and finally, that the *radius* and the third metacarpal bone (popularly called the "cannon bone") form a third angle. These three angles function significantly upward and backward; only the elbow joint can open forward and back. This means that the energy originated by the forward thrust of the hind leg will be transferred to the foreleg's deep muscle system, which moves the shoulder bone and the foreleg up, forward, and back.

The *scapula* is not connected by a joint to the body, but is attached to the chest by two major muscle groups. The forward protraction and backward action are controlled only by the *serratus* muscle. Even the joint of the ankle (metacarpal bone and long pastern) is rather flexible and can bend backward. It is apparent that the foreleg swings forward and back quite freely, and that the bones with muscles and tendons are constructed to receive the energy for support of the forward-shifting weight of the body. Thus we can see that the horse's locomotion originates in the flexion of its hind legs.

Let us next analyze the construction of these hind legs. Unlike the forelegs, they are joined to the body by several joints. This is why they are less flexible than the forelegs. The hind leg is made up of the hip bone and thigh bone *(femur)*, which form a joint that is attached to the *sacrum,* a fusion of five vertebrae. The thigh bone and the *tibia* form another joint—the stifle—and between the *tibia* and the cannon bone we find the hock joint. The cannon bone and long pastern form the fetlock joint, or ankle.

When acceleration begins in the hindquarters, the two main angles create the push, and the hip joint acts as the most positive factor in initiating movement. Apart from the skeleton, and the joints and angles of the hind legs and forelegs, it is evident that we must learn most of all how to influence and control the horse's hind legs—its basic source of locomotion.

The hind legs are connected to the forelegs through the vertebral column. The actions of contraction and extension of the long dorsal muscle lying beside the vertebral column transfer energy through the deep muscles of the shoulder to the muscles of the limbs, but it is the hindquarters that begin the motion. All energy initiated by the thrust of one of the hind legs is transferred to the front legs through these muscles. Every motion is the product of the contraction of one or more muscles. The movements of flexion and extension, and the combination of these movements, produce the various gaits of the animal. Thus the function of the front legs is purely to support the weight of the horse's forward-moving body.

The structure of the horse, showing the functions of its joints and their directions of movement.

General Harry D. Chamberlin, one of America's greatest horsemen, wrote that "The rider must not only be a rider, but a horseman, too, and that requires being familiar with the prominent characteristics of the equine mind." I completely agree that, in order to understand the horse, we must recognize and appreciate its memory and intelligence, its resentment of unjust punishment and appreciation of rewards, and its attentiveness and association of ideas. Without any awareness of these attributes, or of the horse's sensory apparatus (its vision, hearing, and senses of smell and taste), it would always be difficult for us to understand its behavior.

The Memory and Intelligence of the Horse

The horse's memory is excellent, especially for unpleasant things. Of course, memory is not really a function of reason, but rather of the association of ideas, places, and circumstances. That is why we should try to protect the horse from frightening episodes, especially during the early stages of its training.

Our communication with the horse depends upon its memory, for it must learn to recognize the different signals we apply, and remember what they mean. Horses recognize us less by our appearance than by our voices and the manner in which we handle them. When a rider sits on the horse's back, it probably recognizes him; and it is seldom that a horse will hurt its own groom, which also reflects a sense of recognition. We know of many horses that would not let strangers in their stalls—only their grooms. Horses remember their own stalls in the stable and probably even recognize places like racetracks where they have been before. They can also often sense how to find their way back to their stable when they become lost.

As far as their intelligence is concerned, there are divergent opinions. Certainly not all horses are alike, and some are noticeably more intelligent than others. Perhaps we are partly responsible for horses not developing their intelligence to its fullest capacity, as fully as some other animals have. After all, they are usually locked up in the stable, and have human contact only at feeding time or during a short period of exercise; otherwise they are turned out in paddocks, mostly to graze and stand around. They are not handled by humans nearly as much as dogs, many of which may spend virtually all their time in human company. To make objective judgments about the horse's intelligence is thus not easy, but surely horses have at least as much intelligence as most other animals, and almost every horseman can relate a few experiences which testify to the horse's intelligence. And we cannot deny that horses have a certain amount of common sense, along with their good memory and attentiveness. Accordingly, their obedience never totally becomes a reflex.

Vision

The horse's eyes are different from the eyes of most other animals, as well as from human eyes. The position of the eye alone suggests an obvious difference. Human eyes, like those of many animals, are basically frontal, directing the field of vision straight ahead. In contrast, the horse's eyes are located on the sides of its head, thus providing a field of vision that has two sides and sees two separate pictures. Like the human, the horse must focus its eyes on objects ahead, and cannot see to the side or behind at the same time. However, the horse's long neck makes it easy for the eyes to turn in order to observe.

There is not much difference between human vision and the horse's, as far as "blind spots" are concerned. It is a physical fact that when we focus our eyes ahead, there is a space between the object and our position where there exists a blind spot. To eliminate this we must move our head up or down, and so must the horse. Actually, the horse is in a better situation than we are, for its long neck makes it easier for the horse to partly observe what is happening behind it. When approaching a jump, or any sudden change in the level of the ground, the horse first figures out the spot from which to take off, and then judges the height, just as we do.

The horse is supposed to be colorblind, able to see things only in shades of gray. We are not supposed to argue with scientific authorities, and they may well be right. However, while horses may see colors differently than humans do, anyone who rides knows that horses can distinguish between different colors. Riding in the dark we realize that at night they can see as well as cats; they can see—or perhaps feel—where to put their foot. The old cavalryman would simply drop his reins and let the horse take care of him. In the hunting field, galloping horses will jump over a little hole that its rider didn't even notice. Horses can also easily see a strand of wire or rope in the field, and learn to jump it.

How far can the horse see? Perhaps the answer depends upon how interesting or alarming the sight is. Experience suggests that horses can see objects at least several hundred yards away, and much farther if the object is moving. If horses shy, this does not necessarily indicate a problem with their vision; rather, it may be caused by fear of some unknown, unidentifiable object that they can see but not easily associate with what they already know.

Hearing

Hearing is the horse's most fully developed sense. The shape of the ear and its mobility makes horses highly receptive to sound. With its concave shape, the horse's ear is like a little radar saucer, capable of turning very quickly in almost any direction, picking up sounds from great distances. The horse's long neck is also an advantage here, enabling the head to quickly turn in the direction of the sound. The rider often fails to understand a horse's sudden excitement when it has heard a distant but frightening sound.

Horses also learn to recognize certain specific noises, such as the hunting horn or the cavalry bugles of the past. Mild, gentle tones of voice are quieting and encourage confidence; thunderstorms, drum rolls, and shouting cause excitement and often even fear. Interestingly enough, horses will respond to a gunshot even a mile away if they are gun-shy. Horses can also feel ground vibrations through their hooves, and thus recognize the approaching footsteps of man or other animals.

Other Senses

The horse's sense of smell is well developed, and horses hate bad smells! Horses breathe through their nostrils, which is sufficient even when hard breathing is necessary, as in racing. They also smell through their nostrils and can distinguish between different odors and recognize preferred foods, even though they usually cannot identify poisonous foods.

Wartime experiences indicate that horses can smell blood, and of course stallions can smell mares in heat from a considerable distance. They dislike smoke and can readily detect the various medications that must sometimes be mixed into their regular food. On the other hand, some horses are less finicky than others. (It is surprising but true that their taste is very individual.) Almost all horses like salt, sweet flavors, and fresh bark from trees. However, because they are unable to vomit, horses that eat hemlock, yew, and other poisonous plants may die.

It should be mentioned here that horses are panicked by fire and smoke, making it almost impossible to handle them or aid in their escape, as they will normally refuse to go through flames unless trained to do so, like circus horses.

The horse often uses the hairs on its lips, which are very sensitive to touch, to become familiar with unknown objects that they cannot identify visually or through their sense of smell.

The Gaits

At the walk, each of the horse's four legs moves separately, and we hear four distinct hoofbeats as each foot strikes the ground; each hind leg is followed by the foreleg on the same side. In the early stages of training, every second hoofbeat will often sound more strongly, and these will be the front legs. The beats should be equal and regular, and the lengths of strides even. During the walk, the horse's body is always supported by three legs. Its neck and head move slightly up and down and forward. If the hoofbeats do not sound even, the horse is sore on the leg which sounds weaker, and thus the length of the stride will be shorter. In this case, the walk will be irregular, and if the sore leg is a front one, the horse will raise its head to minimize the concussion as that foot hits the ground.

If we watch a horse moving freely in the paddock, we will see that it normally uses the trot as a transition from the walk to the canter, and vice versa. Of the three gaits, the trot is the easiest to explain, for at this gait there are only two beats; the diagonal legs move forward at the same time with even strides and length. As the horse moves from one diagonal to the other, there is also a moment of suspension. Aside from this there are always two hoofs on the ground, thus enabling the horse to balance its body in a straight line. The hind hoofs print in the tracks of the front hoofs at an ordinary trot. The horse's head and neck show no noticeable movement unless it is lame.

In the canter, there are three distinct beats. If the horse is on the left lead, the sequence of the hoofbeats would be: right hind leg; left hind leg together with right front; left front leg. The last beat of the left front leg is the prominent beat, followed by a moment of suspension in which all four legs are in the air, and then the horse comes back to earth again with its right hind leg. At the canter the horse's back swings, and the neck and head are held somewhat higher, the head slightly nodding. The canter is rhythmical, the length of strides even, and the total movement should be harmonious and elastic. If the horse loses its forward impulsion, one will hear and feel four beats instead of three, thus indicating that the canter is incorrect or disunited.

Thus far we have discussed the horse's basic gaits in their simplest form; but there is more to the subject than this, for the ordinary gaits are really only the mid-point of a continuum for each gait that runs from the most compressed or collected form to the most untrammeled or extended form. Since later on the rider must learn to put his horse "on the bit" primarily through transitions from gait to gait, as well as within each gait, this is a good time to establish our terminology with respect to these different variations of the basic gaits.

The collected trot: The horse's diagonal legs are well coordinated, its hocks well engaged.

The Walk

The different walk forms recognized by the International Equestrian Federation (FEI) are the free, medium (ordinary), collected, and extended walks.

In the free walk, the horse is completely free and is permitted to stretch down its neck and head. The medium or ordinary walk is free, regular, calm, and energetic, with hind feet stepping in front of the hoofprints of the forefeet. The horse must be on the bit, and the rider maintains a light contact with its mouth. In the collected walk, the hind legs are more engaged, but touch the ground behind the forefeet, due to the shorter length of the strides. The action becomes higher and more active, though it must remain regular. The horse's neck is raised and arched, its head is almost vertical, and the rider maintains light contact with the mouth. At the extended walk, the horse covers more ground but should not lose its regularity. The hind feet should touch the ground well in front of the hoofprints of the forefeet. The rider retains contact, but the neck of the horse stretches out and the head is carried in front of the vertical.

The collected walk: The horse on the bit, the rider maintaining light contact with its mouth.

The Trot

The trot is the horse's most rhythmical gait, and it is also relatively less tiring than the others; in training it is the most important gait for horse and rider.

There are four different types of trots: working (ordinary) trot, medium trot, collected trot, and extended trot.

The working (also called the ordinary) trot should be lively, energetic, and rhythmical. There must be good hock action, and the hind feet should step on the hoofprints of the forelegs. One should be able to lengthen the stride or shorten it in transition without losing this regularity and rhythm. The neck should be naturally arched and the head carried slightly ahead of the vertical, while the rider maintains a light contact with the bit. In the working trot, the horse can carry the rider for long periods of time without exhaustion, and therefore this trot is generally used for cross-country riding.

The medium trot is a gait between the working and extended trots. The horse goes more forward, and the lengths of the strides become longer but remain regular. The hind feet should touch the ground just past the hoofprints of the forelegs. This is a difficult gait to develop, for it can easily become either too weak and lacking in action, or too irregular and extended.

In the collected trot, the horse covers less ground and its action becomes higher but shorter. The hindquarters become increasingly engaged, the neck more arched, the head almost vertical; the hind feet touch the ground behind the hoofprints of the forefeet. The horse remains on the bit with light contact, and through the action, slows down a little, while impulsion and regularity remain. The collected trot should never be performed for too long a time—for this extreme degree of collection is very hard for the horse to maintain—and should be alternated with freer movements.

In the extended trot, the horse moves with long, elastic, even strides, and covers as much ground as possible. The shoulders swing freely forward, and the hoofprints of the hind legs should fall with a definite overstride in front of those of the forelegs. The hind legs are engaged to the utmost. The frame of the horse lengthens, and its neck and head drop lower and longer, the nose pushing in front of the vertical; there should be slightly firmer contact on the bit. The extended trot is exhausting for the horse, and should only be used for rather brief intervals and on good ground. In general I prefer to execute the various movements at the trot in the posting position. In my opinion there are very few riders today with a seat so secure that he would not disturb the horse's rhythm and balance in the sitting position.

The medium trot, with the horse behind the bit. Note that the head of the horse is two to three inches behind the vertical line.

A correct medium trot: The horse is on the bit with its neck raised and arched properly; its shoulder moves well forward. The rider maintains perfect contact with the horse's mouth.

The canter departure: (Top) The rider's weight already inside, the inside rein slightly loose, the horse's haunches well engaged. (Bottom) The canter lengthens.

The Canter

The following canters are recognized by FEI: working, medium, collected, and extended.

The working canter is a rather energetic, well balanced canter, exhibiting good impulsion, but not short enough to be termed collected. The horse remains on the bit and is quite active with its hock action; thus, it should be able to lengthen the stride without rushing. Also, the horse should be able to make transitions to a shorter stride, while still maintaining a clean, three-beat rhythm. This is the basic canter from which the collected and extended canters are derived.

The medium canter falls between the collected and the extended canters. It is obviously well balanced and characterized by good rhythm. The horse should remain on the bit, but its head may come slightly in front of the vertical. The stride should be long and even. The medium canter should be the ideal standard for the horse in jumping a course.

In the collected canter, an increased engagement of the hindquarters and a shorter length of the stride result in a raised neck with a higher arch. A very light forehand and very active hindquarters are thus characteristic of this canter. A lively impulsion and even rhythm remain, but the horse does not gain much ground. Its lively impulsion must never turn into rushing. The collected canter—also called a steady canter—is invaluable in jumping certain types of fences, as well as in various other circumstances requiring more contact.

The horse's strides will be much longer in the extended canter, but the horse must not lose its calmness and lightness, and must never become hasty. The horse should remain on the bit, but it is allowed a longer and lower neck carriage, so that the tip of its nose points more forward.

In jumping, one of the rider's most important skills is his ability to lengthen his horse's stride without letting the horse become excited, get out of control, or fall on its forehand, leaning on the rider's hands. In many situations the only correct solution to the problem posed by the course designer is for the rider to suddenly extend his horse's stride. Thus, mastering the extended canter is a prime essential for every jumping rider. The rider must of course be able to follow his horse's center of gravity as it moves forward, remaining in perfect balance and control.

It makes no difference whether the rider is interested in jumping, eventing, or dressage riding; all riders must understand the differences between the gaits and the recognized variations that have been described. These are the basic elementary requirements that must be developed one by one, and gradually coordinated with the elementary training movements to be discussed later.

3. How to Sit on a Horse

People talk about many different kinds of seats—the dressage seat, forward seat, balanced seat, crotch seat, normal seat, and so forth. These are all merely labels which convey little real meaning. It should be very simple to describe how to sit on a horse, because there is only one correct way to sit: so that the rider's center of gravity is coordinated with the horse's center of gravity in every situation.

It is unnecessary to confuse the rider with clever catch phrases, or to attempt to create a pseudo-science about how to sit. In fact, there is no essential difference between the dressage, jumping, or cross-country rider's correct seat, and even the jockey's crouch is not an exception. They all have one set of goals in common: to maintain the horse's natural balance, stabilize its rhythm, make it flexible, supple, and relaxed, and thus enable the rider to put the horse on the bit. These must be the objectives of all riders, and all must learn to sit correctly if they are to achieve any of them.

There are no exceptions to this concept of the correct seat. Obviously, the jumping and dressage riders' upper body positions will differ because of their special activities, but the basic principle remains the same. Similarly, the jockey has good reason to sit over the withers of the horse while racing, because of the pronounced forward shift of the horse's center of gravity at the full gallop. Also in the forward and racing seat the rider's weight is not supported entirely on the seat bones—or the crotch triangle —but is mostly distributed throughout his thighs, knees, calves, and partly upon the stirrups in anticipation of the speed at which the horse will be moving. At the other end of the scale, if riders are executing *haute ecole* figures with most of the horse's weight placed on its hindquarters, it is then natural for their position to stay behind the vertical.

The rider's sense of where his center of gravity is in relation to the horse's can be developed and immensely improved upon through practice and special exercises, and especially through riding on the longe line without stirrups. No one is born knowing how to sit on a horse, even though some pupils seem to have an innate talent for finding the right place and the right way to sit, and learn more readily how to follow the horse's movements. Usually these lucky few are also better proportioned physi-

Proper seat and hand position: The rider's shoulder, hip, and heel are in the same vertical line. His knee is flat, his leg behind the girth, his foot in the correct position in the stirrup, with the heel slightly lower than the toes. The elbow is in the front of the hip bone. Hand direction is straight to the horse's mouth.

Lower back position: The rider's pelvis is pushed forward and his shoulder is back.

cally for riding than others, and make quicker progress with seemingly less effort. But no matter how long it takes, everyone must learn to assume the correct seat so that he can use the aids correctly to influence and control the horse. Thus, a correct seat is the foundation for the art of riding.

One precondition for a correct, normal seat is a correctly designed saddle. The deepest point of the saddle should rest above the deepest point of the horse's back: on the muscles directly behind the withers. If this is the case, the rider will be able to sit in the front part of the saddle, as close to the horse as possible, and all the fashionable but superfluous extra padding will be unnecessary.

In a correct seat the weight of the rider is evenly distributed between the two seat bones (which are the lowest bones of the pelvis) and the crotch. These three points form a triangle that affords a stable seat. In addition, the rider also sits partly on the buttocks, and their position determines the position of the legs and torso. The hip bones should be held vertically above the seat bones and never collapse backward.

If the horse is standing on all four legs, and the rider is sitting on three points with his hip bones vertical, the rider's upper body should rest directly above the hip bones in the same vertical line as the horse's center of

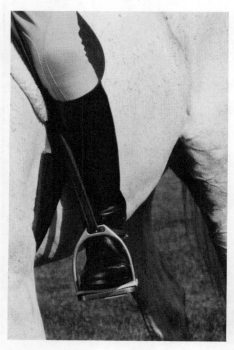

Proper leg and foot position from the front.

Proper leg and foot position from behind: The rider's calf is on the side of the horse; the foot is correct.

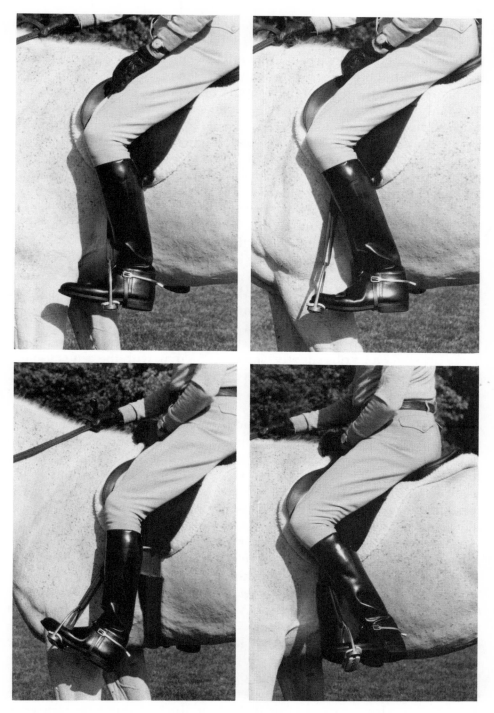

Incorrect leg and foot positions: (Top left) Stirrups too far back, ankle rigid. (Top right) Stirrups on the toes, making it easy to lose the stirrup. (Bottom left) Leg pushed forward; heel is too deep, whole leg rigid. (Bottom right) Leg too far back, with the spur against the side of the horse, irritating it.

gravity. The most comfortable place for the rider to sit is right behind the withers, for there the horse's dorsal vertebrae are fused together. They are rigid, and so initiate no movement by themselves.

The insides of the rider's thighs should be kept flat, covering as much of the sides of the horse's body as is possible. Slim, well-shaped thighs are much to the rider's advantage. They should allow for a firm position and steady contact between the inner part of the knee and the saddle, but without forcing or "pinching." The correct position of the knee gives strong support for the seat. The rider's kneecaps should point forward, if his leg conformation makes that possible, without forcing the knee joint. Tension or stiffness must always be avoided; it is essential for the rider to be able to relax and feel comfortable. The lower legs should rest easily on the horse's ribs, right behind the girth.

It is difficult to specify the correct angle between the rider's thighs and his lower legs, for it depends on the rider's conformation and the relative length of his thighs and lower legs. What is important is that the legs are not pressed, squeezed, or cramped onto the side of the horse. They should rest with a steady, light contact on the ribs. The rider should feel the temperature of the horse through the middle of his calves, and be able to move the skin on its ribs slightly. Constant tapping with the calf is useless, and quickly makes the horse indifferent to normal aids.

The rider should keep his ankles relaxed, soft, and flexible. Stiffness blocks the joints so that no sensitive aids can be applied with the legs, and especially not with the spurs. The ankles must act as shock absorbers.

Though there are many differing opinions regarding the correct position of the foot and heel, there is general agreement that the toes should not be forced to turn unnaturally either inward or outward. Both positions would result in stiffness that would interfere with the correct knee position. The toes should remain in the same natural position in which the rider was built, angled as they are when the rider walks on the flat.

Many horsemen stress the importance of a "deep" heel. However, pressing, pushing, or forcing the heels down result in blocking the ankle joints, stiffening the calves, and pushing the toes forward, thus interfering with sensitive leg signals. Even the seat position changes; the rider starts to sit on the muscles of his buttocks, and his hips drop backward. Instead of pushing the heels down deeply, it is better to *carry* the toes just high enough so that there is no danger of losing the stirrup. The toes should be only one or two inches higher than the heels. The foot should rest with the middle of the sole on the tread of the stirrup, allowing for a springy, elastic movement of the foot between the point of support and the ankle joint. Riding with the stirrup further back on the foot stiffens the action of the leg, while placing it way out on the toes often results in losing the stirrup. A good check on the lower leg position is that when the rider is sitting straight and looking down, his kneecaps should just cover the toes.

Now I will describe the rider's upper body, from the seat bones to the head. In the lower part of the curved spinal column, between the seat bones and hip bones, there are five lumbar vertebrae. Their position and the tightening or softening action of the surrounding muscles of the loin have a significant influence and effect upon the horse's back muscles. Without using this back-muscle action, the hindquarters of the horse can never be truly engaged and, thus, no transitions can be properly executed.

The upper body, supported by the triangle described earlier, is held vertically above the center of gravity of the horse. The shoulders are drawn slightly behind, and not in front of, the hips, keeping the chest naturally round while still soft and relaxed; and the pelvis is pushed forward. The rider's neck and head rest freely in a normal, straight position, with the chin pulled in slightly; this positioning keeps the neck and head natural and supple.

The upper arms "belong" to our upper body. There is no reason to keep them away from the body, suspended in the air. They should rest gently against the rider's body, the elbows relaxing in front of his hip bones and forming a right angle to the forearms. The forearms should point forward in the direction of the horse's mouth.

The hands are held in front and at the center of the upper body, about four inches away from the body, above the horse's withers. They are to be held close together, fingers almost touching, wrists turned inward. Their height depends upon the position of the horse's mouth, which, in turn, depends upon its degree of collection or extension. The position of the hands must be flexible and never fixed, the hands having six to eight inches of play in front of the body. The ideal line is elbow-forearms-hands in one straight line in the direction of the horse's mouth, the reins touching the sides of the neck of the horse. Steady, sensitive contact of the hands with the mouth of the horse can only be maintained if the hands are supported through the forearms by the elbows, which are resting in front of the hip bones. (The best comparison is the waitress carrying a tray loaded with cups of soup. She will stabilize her hands instinctively by holding her elbows close to her sides.)

The hands should turn slightly inward from the wrist, and the rider should be able to see his fingertips when looking down. From this position, the hands can readily make a three- to four-inch movement toward the inside—without moving the elbows—when executing bendings, half-halts, turns, or transitions. And as a final check on position, when the rider is sitting correctly on the horse, his shoulders, hips, and heels should all fall in approximately the same vertical line.

4. The Rider's Aids and Actions

When I think of the rider's aids, I am reminded of an anecdote that is told about one of the world's great pianists, who was asked how difficult it was to learn to play the piano as he did. "It is really not difficult at all," he replied. "You only have to figure out which fingers go on what keys, and for how long. Then you practice for the rest of your life so that you can do it up to tempo."

Communicating with the horse is about the same. It is not really all that difficult to execute the correct instrumental acts once or twice, but it is a lifetime's work to master them. Few horses are really willfully disobedient or stubborn, but any horse will be confused by a rider's clumsy attempts to communicate through an imperfect vocabulary, and this confusion is often mistaken for stupidity or resistance. Luckily, the horse's memory is excellent, as we have noted, and this provides an excellent basis on which to build our communication.

The rider does not only communicate with the horse through direct physical contact; he must also establish a mental and psychological relationship with the horse. In order to achieve this, the rider must be imaginative, skillful, and sensitive; he must patiently explore each animal's individuality, and learn to avoid unnecessary sources of annoyance.

Of course, the rider's physical communication and contact with the horse are still paramount. He gives the orders, and the horse must learn to understand the equestrian language that he employs. This language is often referred to as "aids," though perhaps "signals" would be a more appropriate term for the actions we want to describe.

For communicating with our horses we use *fundamental* and *secondary* aids. The fundamental aids are: the seat and the rider's weight, the legs, and the hands. The secondary aids are: the voice, the whip, the spurs, and reward and punishment.

The Fundamental Communication Aids

The Seat and Weight of the Rider. We can start by discussing the rider's seat and weight, for these are perhaps the most direct means of communication with the horse; an improper seat and poorly distributed weight disturb the horse's balance very profoundly, as mentioned earlier.

Horses, like people, are very sensitive about how they carry weight. In forward movement, our upper bodies must remain in the horse's center of gravity line. We must thus lean forward as the horse's forward motion increases, and shift our weight backward as its motion decreases. In turning to the left or right, our weight must be adjusted laterally, in accordance with the degree of the turn. The natural instinct of the horse is to support the weight it carries evenly, so that it can feel secure and balanced. If we want to make a sharp turn to the right or left, we must put our weight strongly onto our right or left seat bone, and change the position of our legs accordingly. When this is done in a coordinated way, the horse will instinctively turn to the right or left even without any action from the reins.

A secure seat and effective control of weight can best be developed through working on the longe line without stirrups, as will be discussed in greater detail later on.

The Legs. Of equal importance to the rider's weight and balance are the signals given by our legs, for these are the medium that transmit our orders for both forward and lateral movement. Pressure from our legs makes the horse respond in the direction indicated, since the horse's ribs, being covered only with skin, nerves, and very little flesh, are quite sensitive to touch. The intensity of our leg signals can vary from very mild to very strong, from gentle contact to squeezing pressure to sharp nudges or even a kick. The rider's legs rest on the sides of the horse's body and generate the motion. They send the signals that urge the horse to move forward.

We can compare the sensitivity of the horse's ribs to that of our own, and thus our use of leg signals must be carefully controlled. Our execution should never be too strong, yet it should be strong enough to be effective. The intensity of our leg pressure should be applied according to the horse's disposition and training level, and always in the same manner each time in order to get a particular reaction. We should regard our leg aids as signals, not sources of sudden surprise or punishment. They should be used to support and encourage the horse.

Mary Mairs Chapot on Tomboy in London, White City, England, 1964.

Mary Mairs Chapot on White Lightning in Hickstead, England, 1967.

The Hands. Communication through our hands is just as important as that through the seat and leg aids. (One should not rank the respective importance of weight, legs, and hands in communication; their values are of equal significance.)

The hands, through the reins, have two main functions: to control the horse's direction, and to regulate its velocity and gait. Aside from these two functions, the hands also maintain a steady relationship between horse and rider through the reciprocal feeling of the rider's hands and the mouth of the horse; without a perfect continuity of contact, no control can exist. The elastic quality of this rein contact can be compared to that of a rubber band. The reins should remain in steady contact with the mouth, yet with only mild tension and no actual pulling on the mouth. In addition, the reins must never be entirely dropped from the rider's hands, for this completely severs the established relationship.

Coordination of the Rider's Signals. As noted earlier, the fundamental aids provide us with a basic communication network between horse and rider, but it is a mistake to think of any of these basic aids or signals independently of each other; they are all interrelated. It takes coordinated use, guided by the rider's experience and equestrian tact, to produce the most satisfactory results. The art really depends on using all three fundamental aids in consort yet with differing degrees of intensity, so that the horse never becomes either confused or discouraged.

For example, we should never give the signal for increased forward movement with our driving leg aids, while at the same time holding back with the reins, or remaining behind the movement with our weight. The synchronized and coordinated use of our basic aids must be harmoniously and delicately applied.

Maintaining constant control over our body in order always to function or respond correctly is by no means an easy task. We will need concentration, discipline, and dedication—even then, success will not necessarily follow overnight.

The Secondary Communication Aids

The secondary aids of communication are not to be considered substitutes for the fundamental aids of seat, weight, legs, and hands. However, they can be very useful, and their value should not be underestimated.

(Opposite) The rider's style in these photographs is ideal in every respect. The position of the hands and her feeling for the contact with the horse's mouth are exemplary. Her legs are always in the same perfect position. Elegance, coolness, and self-confidence are all evident in these pictures.

The Voice. Though it is obvious that the horse cannot comprehend our spoken language, the human voice can have a considerable value in communication if it is used regularly and with the same tone. It is also true that clicking the tongue, hitting our boots with the whip, or making a sharp crack with the longeing whip, will increase the horse's impulsion and renew its interest, if they are used in moderation and not in a frightening manner. Quiet, low, short, rhythmical sounds, repeated with the same tone, effectively calm down the horse. Music that synchronizes with the natural rhythm of the trot or canter also seems to influence the horse, and can be used as a tool in stabilizing its rhythm. Our voice alone is usually not as effective as when it is employed in conjunction with the other aids.

The Whip. The riding whip should be a regular part of the horseman's equipment. It should be carried at all times—not only on certain occasions—to avoid confusing the horse. We should remember that the whip is primarily a communication aid, and only secondarily a means of punishment. The whip is a tool that can be very usefully employed to teach the horse to better understand the signals of the legs. Therefore it should ordinarily be applied directly behind the rider's boots, and administered only in light taps. Using the whip as punishment is justified only when the animal demonstrates constant resistance, obvious stubbornness, or repeated vices such as kicking, biting, or bucking. Its application in such cases must be short, immediate, and only on the rib cage behind the rider's legs—never, as we have sometimes seen done, on the horse's head!

The Spurs. The spurs are also basic equipment for the rider. They belong on all but the novice rider's boots and, with very few exceptions, should be worn routinely. They too should not be used primarily for punishment, but as a communication aid; they are used for emphasizing the rider's signals and refining the horse's sensitivity. It is obvious that spurs must always be used with great tact and discretion. They should never be stuck clumsily into the horse's ribs; this would be extremely irritating and would result only in resistance. The correct position of the rider's legs will place the spurs parallel, on either side of the horse, lying against its ribs, but *never* turned in *toward* them. If necessary, spurs can be used *against* the ribs with an upward movement, but only in cases of obvious and extreme stubbornness.

Every horse should accept the spurs, which should never be regarded as an enemy. They should be used to emphasize other communication aids,

(Opposite) These pictures demonstrate a perfectly developed and correct style. The rider's upper body is in exactly the same position above the center of gravity of the horse. Very light rein contact with the mouth, elbows and hands deep on the side of the horse's neck, and legs tight on the sides. The spurs never point against the ribs. Concentration, self-confidence, a natural instinct for the proper style, precision, and elegance are obvious in both pictures.

William C. Steinkraus on Snowbound in Hickstead, England, 1967.

William C. Steinkraus on Snowbound in Aachen, Germany, 1970.

not to merely irritate. The horse's acceptance of the spurs will depend upon the rider's tact and experience. It is commonly believed that mares object to spurs, but experience has taught me that if they are used in a proper, careful manner, mares too will learn to accept them.

Reward. The human traits of generosity and understanding function as highly desirable qualities in a rider or trainer. For if we encounter misunderstandings or problems with a horse, the wisest approach is always to analyze the situation with patience and understanding.

The physical affection and appreciation that humans demonstrate with a pat on the shoulder certainly does not hurt, and can be applied similarly to animals. A short pat of appreciation by the rider is readily understood by the horse. Such rewards have great positive psychological value, and the rider should be generous in using them. Patting on the neck, dismounting, offering carrots or sugar, and making soft, appreciative sounds, are all at our disposal. Obviously, however, these rewards cannot be used as bribes in an attempt to solve problems. For instance, if the horse fails to cooperate, and uses its power and strength in stubborn refusal to accept properly given aids, then the rider must be firm, and the use of punishment, tempered with common sense, is justified.

Punishment. There is a limit to how long punishment should be continued or how often repeated. The rider must attempt to educate the horse, and try to make it understand his signals. However, if one encounters repeated disobedience, then a measured, controlled physical punishment must immediately follow the horse's unjustified resistance or bad behavior. The rider should never lose his temper, and after a few short, firm strokes with the whip, can even resort to patting the neck of the horse, thus reaffirming his continued friendship. When punishment is prolonged and cruel, the animal no longer understands why it is being administered; it only feels the pain. An experienced rider seldom needs to use punishment. Analyzing the problem and learning the reasons for the horse's misbehavior will often prove better substitutes.

We should remember that unjust punishment will surely be answered with resentment. We must be sure that the horse's bad behavior was not the result of our own confused communication. Jerking the horse's mouth as punishment is seldom or never a good tactic, and in fact, its effect will often be contradictory. Punishment of horses should, in most cases, be handled as we would deal with a naughty child. Remember, too, that in many cases, physical pain or discomfort eventually prove to be the source of the horse's apparent opposition; ill-fitting tack, or even impending lameness or illness have often been mistaken for resistance.

An old adage seems highly applicable here: *When the knowledge of riding comes to an end, abuse and cruelty begin.*

The Rider's Actions at the Walk

The rider's signal for the horse to start walking is pressure of his lower legs on the sides of the horse, against the ribs. This pressure must be supported by a forward-driving seat, which is to say, by pushing forward the crotch and pelvic bones, and supporting them with the lower part of the spinal column. This combination of aids—known as the braced back—should be used to start all movements and to initiate all transitions. As the back braces, the muscles in the rider's fingers and wrist relax, while the fingers retain soft contact with the bit, and follow the horse's mouth in its forward movement. The horse must feel that the "door is open."

The upper body follows the forward motion and synchronizes with it. The rider sits deeply in the saddle on his seat bones so that he can feel each one move forward as the shoulder of the horse on that side moves forward. (Using the right side as an example, the right seat bone moves forward, pushed by the off hind leg, followed immediately by the left seat

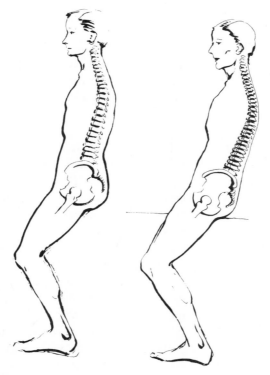

The braced-back function: Pushing the lower part of the spine forward has a great influence on the engagement of the hindquarters.

bone being moved forward, pushed by the near hind leg.) This sequence of movements of the seat bones gives the rider a feeling for the regularity, evenness, and length of the horse's strides. The rider must feel the movements of his seat bones and recognize the moment when each hind leg has pushed off and is in the air. If the rider wishes to increase the horse's impulsion, lengthen its stride, or influence the hind leg's direction, his leg signals are applied more effectively at this moment of suspension. After all, the leg of the horse which is on the ground must support both part of its own distributed weight, and that of the rider—it is not free at that moment to respond to leg signals given by the rider.

The rider, sitting correctly and feeling the horse's hind-leg movement through his seat, should be able to dictate an even rhythm by applying a rhythmical pressure to the sides of the horse through the calves of his legs.

Looking down with a slight tilt of his head, the rider will notice that after one of his seat bones has moved forward, along with the horse's shoulder, the same shoulder moves immediately backward. It is at this moment that the rider's leg should add a slight pressure to that side of the horse, encouraging the thrust of its hind leg, which will follow.

The Rider's Actions at the Trot

As we have stated, in trotting, one pair of diagonal legs moves forward together, followed by the other pair of diagonal legs, and we feel and hear only two beats on the ground. There are two different ways of riding to the trot. One is by posting (rising) to the trot, and the other is by remaining in the sitting position.

Rising/Posting Position. Every elementary training movement can be executed from the posting trot. (However, the rider with a well-developed seat can be even more effective by using the sitting trot to influence the horse in these elementary movements.) In the rising position, the weight of the rider is supported primarily by his knees, while the rest of his weight is distributed throughout his thighs and calves, with some weight (though not a significant amount) resting in the stirrups. The rider's upper body—especially his seat bones and hips—moves forward in the direction of the withers, close to the saddle, alternately using one of the hind leg's thrusting impulses. The whole forward movement of the upper body is in synchrony with one of the diagonal pairs of legs, and when a hind leg touches the ground, the rider softly lowers his seat into the saddle. This action must be elastic, soft, and in perfect timing with the hind leg touching the ground.

Through his forward-moving upper body—or more accurately, through the rise and fall of his seat—the rider should be able to dictate to the horse the required rhythm. When his seat touches down into the saddle, the rider's driving legs (calves) should tighten against the sides of the horse. His rising movement must synchronize with the forward swing of one of the horse's shoulders, his seat returning to the saddle when the opposite hind leg touches the ground. Almost no muscular energy is involved in posting, since the rider uses the hind leg's thrust for his upper body's rising movement and lets gravity (filtered through the knees) effect his return to the saddle. Thus, the "rising" trot should never be tiring, either for the rider or the horse, and should be capable of being continued endlessly. It is also the easiest way for the horse to travel long distances under the rider's weight. When using a posting trot, the rider should change the diagonal quite often; otherwise the horse will become stiff on one side, and the supporting pair of diagonal legs (especially the hind leg) will become overstrained. Both diagonals should be equally developed.

The Sitting Trot. The sitting trot is more difficult to perfect and is used by more advanced and developed riders. To sit to the trot, the rider must follow the up-and-down swinging movements of the back of the horse smoothly, so that he can retain the proper position. The horse's back muscles *(longissimi dorsi)* will remain relaxed only if the rider's seat smoothly follows the rhythm of the horse. When such is the case, the horse will accept the rider's weight and will not harden or stiffen his back in resistance to it, allowing the rider to sit comfortably. If the horse has thus accepted the rider's seat, then the rider's body, too, can remain relaxed; all his muscles can remain soft and follow the horse's back movement without any discomfort. The rider's upper body should remain erect and yet not stiff; by pushing the stomach slightly forward, the rider can avoid any backward collapse of the hips. The seat bones should never budge from the back of the horse, and both legs should cling, easily and without force, in the correct position on the ribs of the horse.

When the sitting trot is correctly performed, the rider can breathe normally, talk, and even rotate his upper body from the hips in either direction, without changing his position below the hips. Unquestionably, the rider's aids can be applied more effectively and sensitively in the sitting trot, assuming that he has developed such a secure seat that maintaining it does not interfere with the forward-driving action of the legs, or the steady contact of his hands.

The Rider's Actions at the Canter

Before we discuss the rider's actions at the canter, it is very important to understand how to canter-on, or make the strike-off into the canter. Even before the strike-off, the horse first needs a warning—a half-halt—to make it alert and prepare it, both mentally and physically, to accept the canter-on signals. The rider should sit with his weight slightly on his outside seat bone, and maintain a slight inside bending of the horse around his tight inside leg on the girth, holding back with both reins in the direction of his outside hip. Then he must apply pressure with both legs at the same time, but more actively with the outside leg behind the girth. When the horse starts the departure movement, contact on both reins relaxes; the inside hand moves forward with the horse's inside shoulder, while the outside hand maintains a light contact with its mouth.

When the horse strikes off to the canter movement, its inside shoulder must be free; otherwise the horse will fall into a false lead (cross-canter) behind. Be careful not to let the inside hand interfere with the inside corner of the horse's mouth in the air during the transition to the canter, for this would interfere with the freedom of the inside shoulder. The horse should never be bent outward at the strike-off.

It is advisable at first to make the transition to the canter from the trot. After the first cantering stride, the rider must shift his weight back to his inside seat bone. His inside leg then continues to elicit and support every stride, while his outside leg controls any deviation of the hindquarters.

The rider's inside leg elicits movement at every stride, while his outside hand simultaneously asks the horse to wait and wait. The inside hand keeps only the slightest contact and is always ready to give generously, preserving only the direction. The rider's seat must follow the back of the horse with a soft movement, while the rider thinks "forward and down."

The canter gives the rider the feeling of three beats—or three phases—and thus is distinctly different from the other gaits. Perhaps this gait is the easiest for the horse as well as for the rider, for it is a swinging, rhythmical movement.

In the canter, the horse's shoulders rise, as one of its hind legs, carrying the whole weight of its body, thrusts off. Then follows a moment of suspension, as the hindquarters rise while the leading foreleg touches down, eventually overtaking the support. In analyzing the canter, we must discuss the diagonal support that should exist between the rider's inside leg and his outside hand. This diagonal support also exists in the other gaits, but it is not as clearly pronounced as at the canter.

By definition, the inside of the horse is the direction in which it is bent, while the outside is the opposite. Bearing in mind that almost no horse is completely straight in its body, we still must establish a frame of reference in the canter, just as in the other gaits, in which the body and forward movement will remain straight.

To achieve this, the inside leg supports and dictates the degree of impulsion, which is steadily controlled by the contact of the outside hand. The inside hand maintains the required direction, yet remains ready to be generously yielding, never holding back the forward-moving leading shoulder. The outside leg, positioned a little behind the inside leg, rather passively prevents the outside hind leg from deviating from the straight line.

The rider sits deeply with his seat bones, and the sensation of the seat and lower part of the back is such that they are rhythmically drawn *down and forward, down and forward . . .* and so forth. The feeling can be compared with sitting in a rocking chair. When the inside seat bone and hip are moving forward in relation to the outside seat bone and hip, the rider must be careful to insure that his outside shoulder and hip remain parallel to the horse's shoulders, and are not left behind. The inside leg's supporting action at every stride must be felt and simultaneously controlled on the opposite side by the outside hand. These actions will keep the horse straight, collected, round, and well balanced.

Knowing how to sit on a horse physically and how to communicate with it through the aids is not enough. Both must be practiced and studied at length, and it will still take a long time for these actions to develop into automatic, instantaneous habits within the rider's body.

Practice and repetition are necessary to develop synchrony with the swinging movement of the horse's back. Even more practice is necessary in order to learn to follow these movements while remaining relaxed, supple, and erect with the upper body, keeping the lowest part of the spine in its original position without letting it collapse backward. Remember that it is only in this erect position that the vertebrae can readily be tightened into a correct braced back, or relaxed. These actions have a great influence on the back muscles of the horse, but the rider's seat cannot be effective if he is unaware of this fact, or unable to make use of it. The rider must also be aware of the leg movements of the horse, and feel through his seat when the horse's feet leave the ground and are in the air, not supporting any weight. If the rider does not develop this awareness, his aids—due to faulty timing—will never produce optimal results.

All these physical feelings are interrelated with the rider's mental understanding of the horse. Horses vary as much as humans do, and so do their surrounding circumstances. The individual temperaments and dispositions of different horses must always be taken into consideration. The rider's evaluation of his horse's ability and its level of intelligence should govern his actions.

The rider must constantly ask himself: Are patience and rewards, or firmness and punishment more appropriate in this particular situation? "Equestrian tact" is less concerned with physical abilities than with psychological attributes. Mutual understanding depends not only upon the horse, but also upon the rider's disposition and mental attitude.

5. The Basic Training of the Horse

The International Equestrian Federation (FEI) states that the object of dressage—the training of the horse— "is the harmonious development of the physique and ability of the horse. As a result it makes the horse calm, supple, loose and flexible, but also confident, attentive and keen, thus achieving perfect understanding with his rider." I agree with that statement entirely. Such a horse is not fighting with its rider and resisting his domination, but willingly accepting the relationship with him. In other words, the horse is willing to try to understand and follow its rider's communication; it is supple when carrying its rider's weight, obedient when restrained, and eager (yet not excited) when urged forward.

Advanced horse training is often highly specialized. In the earlier stages, however, it makes no difference whether the horse will eventually be used for competitive dressage, jumping, eventing, or simply pleasure riding; its basic foundation of training should be the same. Only later does the training become more specific for the discipline in which the horse will specialize.

Every horse should learn to go "on the bit," through the mechanism of the half-halt, and through transitions between and within the basic gaits; and every horse should learn to perform certain basic training movements that will develop the flexibility and suppleness of its body and the rider's control over it. It is my hope that what follows will help riders to accomplish this, so that they can go on to address whatever other challenges in equestrian sport they choose to accept.

(Opposite) Though these pictures were taken on different horses and in different places, the rider's upper body is always in the same perfect position above the center of the horse. His hands and elbows are deep on the sides, always in correct contact and never disturbing the horse. The horses are on the bit above the fences. The rider's upper body remains close to the horse, even though his seat is somewhat high above the saddle.

Frank D. Chapot on Viscount in the Montreal Olympics, 1976.

Frank D. Chapot on San Lucas in Aachen, Germany, 1962.

Transitions

The training of the horse begins with changing from one gait to another —from stand-still to walk, walk to trot, trot to canter, and vice versa. These changes of gait and speed are called transitions.

At the beginning, transitions must be practiced very gradually; the confusion so often created by tactlessly performed transitions will then prove avoidable. The young horse needs time to understand the rider's aids for any change of gait or speed. Well-coordinated signals for transitions will make a big difference in the success of the more demanding training movements that will be introduced to the horse later.

A gentle, carefully applied leg signal can be supported by the use of the voice, or a light touch with the whip on the horse's side, right behind the rider's boots. Even patting the horse with one's hand in the same place touched with the whip will usually be understood.

As training continues, the aids for transitions are applied more quickly, though still smoothly. An harmonious rhythm in the new gait must be established as soon as possible. Once the horse understands simple, gradual transitions—from walk to trot and trot to canter, and vice versa—it can be trained to make such bigger transitions as from walk to canter, canter to walk and rein-back, rein-back to canter, and full-halt to trot or canter. There are many variations which will clearly reveal the rider's skill in coordinating his aids.

Practicing transitions develops the rider's coordination of communication. Energetic upward transitions, without rushing or increasing the rhythm, and smooth, fluid downward transitions, without losing the rhythm, are true evidence of good training. During all these transitions, the position of the horse's head and neck should remain the same.

The Half-Halt

Nobody likes to be surprised. Before human athletes are asked to do something new, their coach explains to them what he expects and how to perform it. With animals, it is not so simple. We will obtain the best results with horses if, before we request any new movement, we give them a warning that a signal is about to follow. This warning is called—in equestrian terminology—the half-halt. (Internationally, it is often referred to by its German name, the half-*parade.)*

The half-halt is initiated with the driving aids. The rider's seat, activated by a braced back and driving legs that press forward on both sides somewhat behind the girth, produces more engagement of the hindquarters. At the same time, the hands resist with tightened finger and forearm muscles, while still remaining in their original position. As soon as the horse readjusts its balance in response to these actions, the fingers relax, and the forward-driving seat is again permitted to predominate. These three actions—driving forward, retarding the motion, and then resuming the forward drive—if executed with good coordination, will produce the desired results.

The half-halt, as the expression indicates, never intends to bring the horse to a full halt. It is a signal made by the coordinated action of the rider's seat, legs, and hands. One of its main purposes is to increase the horse's attention and make him alert. Other objectives are to decrease speed, to renew and increase collection without losing impulsion, and to regulate the horse's rhythm and balance. A correctly executed half-halt helps to shift more weight to the horse's hindquarters, resulting in more engagement of its hind legs and a lightening of its contact with the rider's hand, if needed. In short, a properly executed half-halt improves the horse's posture within the gait.

As we have already emphasized, no horse can maintain impulsion and rhythm by itself. It takes the rider's driving aids, combined with periodic half-halts, to keep the horse together in a lively rhythm, in light contact with the rider's hand, and to put and keep it on the bit. The action of the half-halt also has a regulating and refining effect that enables the horse to make fluent transitions from one movement to another.

The half-halt: The seat, braced back, and driving legs press forward to engage the hindquarters. Simultaneously, the hands and arms resist, and then relax.

Putting the Horse on the Bit

Almost every instructor tells his pupils to "put the horse on the bit." Indeed, there is general agreement that being "on the bit" is highly important, that it is a very special feeling, and that riding is easier and more pleasant when the horse is on the bit. All that is true; and when one *can*, in fact, put the horse on the bit, he is certainly an experienced rider. Yet despite the importance of this subject, we very seldom find a clear explanation of it in writing, or even firsthand from our instructors.

So let me first describe what it looks like when the horse is on the bit. The feeling and appearance of this condition are the same in all gaits: the horse is in perfect natural balance and is straight in its body; its neck is to some degree elevated and arched, the highest point being the poll between attentive ears; and its profile lies a couple of inches in front of the vertical. The hindquarters are drawn somewhat under its body, closer to the center of gravity. The muscles in its jaw, neck, back, loin, and haunches are all

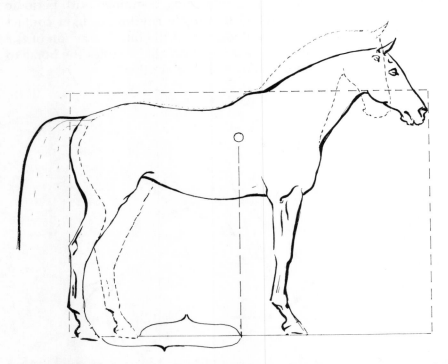

The dotted line shows the change in the horse's frame when it is on the bit. Note that the hind legs move closer to the center of gravity.

soft and relaxed. The rider has only a light contact with the horse's mouth, which is closed; the horse is not playing with the bit, though it may be calmly chewing on it. Even standing still, the horse gives the impression that it is ready and willing to move forward. Full harmony in relaxation is perhaps the primary characteristic.

The ultimate objective of the rider's own development, as well as the goal of the horse's training, is being able to put the horse on the bit. The horse can avoid it in two ways. It can easily get either *behind the bit* or *above the bit,* in both cases resisting the rider's influence.

Getting *behind the bit* results mostly from the rider trying to decrease the horse's speed by strongly pulling back on its mouth with the reins. It is easy for the horse to bend its head between the first two cervical vertebrae, curve its neck, and draw its chin back to its chest. If it succeeds in getting into that "over-bent" position, the rider has lost all control. The hindquarters will then fail to be engaged at all, and it will feel as if two thirds of the horse's body is behind the rider's seat, for the horse's center of gravity will move forward. As a result, the horse gets completely on the forehand, accelerates faster and faster to retain its balance, and tries more and more to find support in the rider's hand. Dropping behind the bit can become a habit which represents real trouble for the rider, for it can be very difficult to correct.

Getting *above the bit* is another way for the horse to resist. In this case the horse raises its head to avoid contact with the rider's hand. It is usually unwilling to accept this contact because it is afraid of the rider's hand; quite possibly the horse's mouth has been hurt earlier in its training, and now it raises its head in an effort to defend itself. Of course, in this position the hindquarters cannot either be engaged or controlled by the rider's aids. The horse can run and fight against the rider, and the rider will not be able to keep his legs on the sides of the horse—they will not be accepted and will be "thrown away." The horse can be put on the bit more readily from above the bit than from behind the bit, but the rider must have a well-developed, independent seat, and completely independent hands in order to establish correct contact with the horse's mouth and have his legs accepted.

To put a horse onto the bit, one must start slowly and gradually; otherwise it is very easy to put the horse behind the bit. Light contact should first be established with quite long reins. Gradually the driving aids are increased until the horse stretches out its neck to reach the bit, which occurs only when it finds the correct contact. The rider then proceeds by alternating between half-halts, shortening the stride, driving again, and repeating the half-halts, while gradually taking more contact with shortened reins. The rider's forward-driving seat and legs maintain the horse's liveliness and impulsion, as its hind legs become more engaged and move

Putting the horse on the bit through gradually increased contact and forward drive; moving onto the bit from a medium walk.

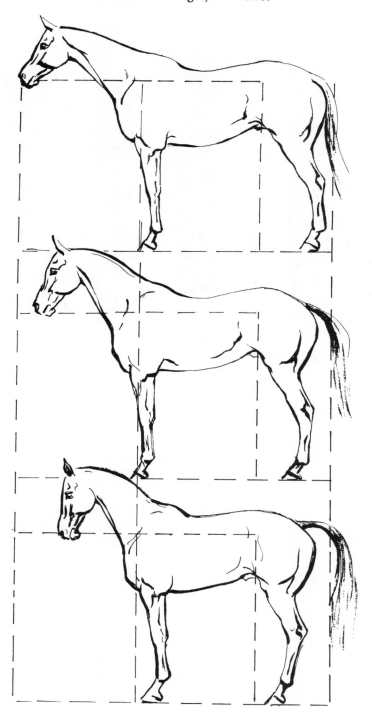

Three different stages of collection, from the horse in repose to the horse that is on the bit.

Robert Ridland on Almost Persuaded in Lucerne, Switzerland, 1974.

closer to the center of gravity. (Of course, they never actually reach a point on the ground directly under the center of gravity, but their tendency should strive in that direction.) The hindquarters lower and actually sink, making it possible for the hocks to reach forward, which is possible only if the spine is raised from the original position. This changes the spaces between the horse's vertebrae; they become more open and separated, and the spinal column becomes more elastic and springy. As a result, the arch of the horse's neck rises, as does the position of its head, while the back and side muscles become relaxed. The strides become somewhat shorter and more elevated, and the rider's contact with the horse's mouth becomes as light as a feather. Within this framework, the horse is very sensitive to all aids, and well disposed both mentally and physically to receiving the rider's signals. In general, this description holds true for all gaits.

The frame of the whole horse on the bit, including the arch of the neck and position of the head, depends upon its conformation. This means that the horse can be very satisfactorily on the bit, yet without a very elevated, curved neck and high head position, so long as it is well balanced in accordance with its body. This is to say that it is not on the forehand, it accepts light hand contact, it is composed in its body, and is eagerly sensitive and receptive to do whatever is requested through the rider's aids.

Robert Ridland on Blue Plum in Aachen, Germany, 1970. Nice harmony and rein contact, but the seat should be closer to the horse's back.

Even a short, low-necked horse with a long back and loins can be put on the bit, despite its many conformation faults. However, this will require a better rider and a longer time to succeed, and the horse will never give the full impression described earlier, which applies best to horses of good or ideal conformation.

The Halt

The halt must be practiced systematically, but not too often. There is a big difference between merely stopping a horse that is in motion and making a correct full halt. In the correct halt, the horse must be attentive and still, straight in its body and collected in position, its own weight and the rider's distributed equally on all four legs. The horse must remain on the bit, with an elevated and arched neck position, its nose slightly in front of the vertical, and with light contact being maintained by the rider's hand. In preparation for the halt, repeated half-halts should be used, so that the pace is reduced through a smooth transition, gradually leading to the halt. The rider's seat, legs, and hands, applied simultaneously, ensure the engagement of the horse's hind legs and preserve its balance. The rider's back-muscle action is essential, for without this aid, the halt would

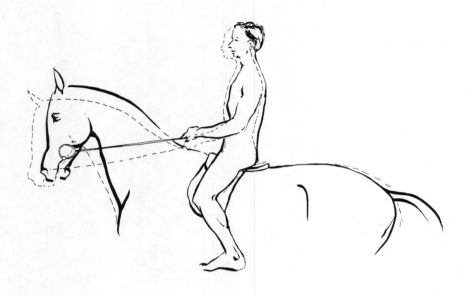

The halt: Note the horse's elevated and arched neck, with its nose slightly in front of the vertical. The rider's back is braced and his hand rises to preserve a straight line to the bit.

be only a pull on the reins. The halt should only be performed when the horse is on the bit. Once it is complete, the rider must relax, applying no pressure anywhere.

A slight advance of the hands and slight backward motion of the upper body will prevent any backward step once the horse has halted. With advanced training the horse should be able to stop from any gait into a perfectly straight position. The distance it takes to come to full stop will always depend upon the degree of the training level of the horse, as well as the rider's skill.

Well-executed halts are the best preparation for the short turns which are so necessary on the jumping course, especially in jump-offs. Correct halts improve the bending of the hind legs three joints, which is necessary if the horse is to make a sudden backward shift of its center of gravity. (It would be a mistake not to also recognize the significance of this important fact in relation to the horse's take-off at a jump.)

After a well-executed halt, the rider should feel that two thirds of the horse's body is in front of his seat bones, and that the horse is ready to move off immediately into any gait or movement, whatever the rider should request.

6. The Essential Training Movements

As soon as the horse is moving well at the basic gaits, can make simple transitions, and can carry itself more or less on the bit with good balance and impulsion, it should be introduced to certain basic training movements, which will facilitate and accelerate its further development. Every training program must, of course, be adapted to each individual horse. However, there are some movements which are necessary *in principle,* and which cannot be ignored in any training program. Also, it is not practical to introduce certain movements in the wrong sequence, for many of them are especially valuable as preparation for those that follow. There is, therefore, a basic, common-sense progression to follow, that can serve as a general guide for anyone involved in training nearly any kind of riding horse. We will discuss these essential training movements in detail in the following sequence, which is in general the order in which they should be introduced:

1. Leg-Yielding
2. Turn on the Forehand
3. Rein-Back
4. Shoulder-In
5. Haunches-In, Haunches-Out
6. Turn on the Haunches
7. Half-Pass on Two Tracks
8. Counter-Canter and Flying Change of Lead

Leg-Yielding

Leg-yielding is one of the most important basic exercises. It is a lateral movement that helps to make the horse supple and obedient, and also a key to preparing the horse for such other elementary movements as the shoulder-in, half-pass, and travers and renvers. Another great benefit of leg-yielding is that it teaches the horse to accept the rider's legs against its

Leg-yielding to the right: (Left) The rider's weight is slightly inside with the horse bent to the right, its right foreleg over the left. (Right) The right hind leg is crossing in front of the left hind leg.

sides, and to understand that when the rider's legs push sideways, one of its hind legs should cross over in front of the other hind leg.

When leg-yielding to the right (for example), the horse should be slightly bent to the right at the poll, and the rider should see only the horse's eyebrow and nostril. He should put more weight on his right seat bone when starting, then sit in the middle and—with right leg pressure—help the horse's right hind leg to move in the opposite direction of its bending, crossing in front of the left hind leg. The right time for the rider to squeeze is always when the horse's hind leg leaves the ground. Instinctively the horse's right foreleg will cross in front of the other foreleg. In leg-yielding, the horse always moves in a direction *opposite* to that toward which it is bent, and its inside legs cross in front of its outside legs.

Leg-yielding can be practiced by moving away from the long side, along the long side, across a diagonal, or on a circle, and is taught first at walk and later at trot. Should the horse move more laterally than is desired, it must immediately be ridden forward, using both legs. Maintaining the rhythm and impulsion is important, and the horse should not be over-bent. The outward swing of the haunches can be controlled by the rider's outside leg, supported by the inside rein. Practicing leg-yielding exercises

Leg-yielding to the left: The photograph shows the hind legs crossing. The rider's rein contact is very light, just enough to avoid having the right shoulder fall out.

Leg-yielding from behind: The left hind leg moves to cross the right one.

develops the horse's obedience and suppleness while helping teach it to accept the bit.

Turn on the Forehand

The turn on the forehand is a basic exercise that is closely related to leg-yielding in that its primary purpose is to teach the horse to obey lateral leg and rein controls. It also helps to supple the horse and improve his obedience to the aids. The aids are the same as in leg-yielding, except that instead of going forward, the horse moves around its inside foreleg—which continues stepping all the time, rather than pivoting—as its hind legs move sideways, the inside hind leg crossing over in front of the outside hind leg. The horse is definitely bent to the inside, and at the beginning of the exercise the weight of the rider may be shifted to the outside, in the direction toward which the turn is made; the horse will support the excess weight as it steps to the side. The outside rein prevents forward motion and keeps the outside shoulder straight, while the rider's outside leg controls the steps to prevent acceleration.

Rein-Back

In the rein-back the horse steps backward. Its legs move in the same sequence as the trot, with the diagonal pairs of legs moving at almost the same time. (We should really hear two hoofbeats, though occasionally one will hear four.) The horse should not drag his feet, but should lift them well; and it must remain in a straight line and not hurry.

The rein-back is a delicate exercise that must be handled with patience, for at the beginning, many horses resist. Therefore, as a rule, rein-back signals should be given only if the horse is on the bit—or at least not above the bit—and should never be started unless the horse is standing squarely on all four legs. Never force the rein-back. If the rider meets resistance, he must immediately ride forward a few strides and then try again. The horse should rein-back step by step, never moving hastily, and should be willing to proceed forward immediately when asked by the rider.

To move backward, the weight of the rider should be shifted to the front part of the seat bones without pressure. Then an increased restraining action is initiated with one rein, supported by leg pressure on the same side. The rider yields immediately as the horse begins its backward movement, and repeats the same action on the other side, calmly following each action backward, step by step in a slow sequence. In the rein-back, the horse's neck must not be forcefully shortened by pulling on the reins. The horse should move its diagonal pairs of legs in a walking rhythm. The rider must remain in steady, light contact with the horse's mouth, and follow it backward with his hands, just as he follows it in the forward movement. Once the horse has learned the rein-back signals, the rider should ask for a certain number of strides in backing, and must feel it in his seat when each hind leg moves.

When the foreleg and its shoulder move backward, the hind leg movement on that side follows backward instantly. The horse must be taught to make only as many strides as the rider indicates, and to move forward in any gait immediately afterward. When the rider's upper body shifts slightly back, and his braced back and both legs urge the horse forward, the hands "open the door" at the same time, and the upper body follows the movement forward. The turn on the forehand is good preparation for the rein-back movement.

It is a good idea to start teaching the horse to back while standing beside an arena wall or fence. Bending the horse slightly to the inside while keeping the inside leg a little behind the girth will help assure that the horse remains straight in the backward motion. If the horse resists the signals to back, the rider should not attempt to force it to back straight. The main objective should be to move, *somehow,* the hind legs out of their position of resistance. After repeating this exercise several times, the horse will start to step backward a little, and later the lateral movement will gradually become smaller, allowing for straight backing to be achieved.

Do not hesitate to use the exercise of alternating backward and forward movement. If controlled, this is an excellent demonstration of the rider's coordinated aids and the horse's complete understanding of the rider's communication. It is proof of the horse's suppleness and the bending of the joints of its hind legs. It also proves that the action of the rein is going through the body, and not stopping at the neck.

Shoulder-In

Most experts agree that the shoulder-in is the most important exercise of all the lateral movements. It is used to make the horse straight, to improve its suppleness and obedience, and also to increase the engagement of the hindquarters. It is obvious that the shoulder-in developed from leg-yielding. The only difference is that the bending position is opposite, and the legs do not cross each other.

According to historians, La Guérinière (who died in 1751) should be credited with perfecting the shoulder-in, though an earlier form was practiced by the Duke of Newcastle (1592–1676).

To perform the shoulder-in, the outside foreleg of the horse is brought *in,* and placed in front of the inside hind leg. The angle should be about thirty degrees, with the horse being bent around the inside leg of the rider. The horse's movement is forward and the legs do not cross each other. This position creates three parallel tracks: the outside hind leg moves forward alone; next to it, and about one-and-a-half feet away, is the track of the inside hind leg and outside foreleg, moving together; and finally, parallel to the other two lines, is the track of the inside foreleg.

Observing a correct shoulder-in from the front or from behind, the inside hind leg and outside foreleg will appear to cover each other, as they move on the same track. The inside hind leg steps well underneath the weight of the horse, which is one of the big differences between leg-yielding and the shoulder-in. The horse must bend its body in its ribs, something it would not otherwise do, in order to maintain its impulsion and rhythm. The rider's primary concern should be to prevent the outside hind leg from stepping out.

In the shoulder-in, the horse does not look in the direction in which it is moving. When the rider brings the forehand toward the inside through the action of both reins, he first puts more weight on his outside seat bone, and then sits in the center, or slightly inside; he maintains the bending with the inside rein and counterbalances it with the outside rein, thus both preventing the outer shoulder from falling out and leading the horse in the desired direction. His inside leg maintains the forward drive of the inside hock, and his outside leg prevents the deviation of the outside hind leg.

The shoulder-in exercise is a fine test of the rider's coordination in using the aids. In principle, he should support the horse equally with both reins and legs, but sometimes he must become lighter or stronger, depending upon the reaction of the horse. The shoulder-in improves the bending of all three joints of the horse's hind leg and teaches it to become more

Shoulder-in to the right: Perfect execution, with the right hind leg covered by the left foreleg.

Shoulder-in to the right: The horse moves on four tracks.

responsive to the rider's leg and rein aids. The horse learns to move forward and sideways in the correct lateral position and to maintain its regular tempo.

The shoulder-in should be practiced first at a walk, and later on at a collected trot, for at the walk the impulsion can easily be lost.

Finally, it must be mentioned here that there is some controversy regarding the doctrines of the shoulder-in. There are differing opinions as to the correct degree of the angle of the horse from the straight line. If the angle is more than thirty degrees—say forty-five degrees or even more—the track will show four hoofprints instead of only three. This forty-five degree angle is still practiced by the Spanish Riding School; however, when performed by less experienced riders, both the sequence of paces and, even more important, forward movement often suffer.

Haunches-In, Haunches-Out

Haunches-in (also called *travers)*, and haunches-out (called *renvers)* are less used than the more important training movements. Some experts believe that horses, in general, have a tendency to become crooked anyway, and therefore it is better not to teach a position which is very close to crookedness. I disagree with that argument, provided that the exercises are properly executed.

Both the travers and renvers are lateral exercises that are actually helpful in correcting crookedness, as well as obtaining more bending of the hind legs and increasing obedience to the rider's leg aids. For jumpers it is excellent preparation for making sharp turns, almost on the spot.

During haunches-in, which is closely related to the shoulder-in, the horse is bent around the rider's inside leg. The forehand moves straight forward on the track, and the hindquarters are bent to the inside. The outside hind leg steps over and in front of the inside one, in response to pressure from the rider's outside leg behind the girth. The lateral bending is regular from head to tail.

The haunches-out can be described as the opposite of the haunches-in. In this exercise, however, the hindquarters remain in the track while the forehand position is just as it would be in the shoulder-in; however, in the renvers the horse looks in the direction in which it is moving. The rider's outside leg on the girth is the more active one, in order to produce lateral bending; his inside leg makes the horse step sideways. The rider's weight should be on his outside seat bone. Both these movements are useful, but they should not be practiced for too long a period at once, nor too frequently.

Haunches-in: The horse's forelegs and hind legs move straight forward, and do not cross each other. The hindquarters are correctly off the line.

Turn on the Haunches

The turn on the haunches is similar to the turn on the forehand, except that it is executed around the hindquarters of the horse. This is an exercise that should only be taught at a walk. It is widely acknowledged as the most helpful schooling movement in developing influence and control over the hindquarters of the horse. In jumping competition, it is the best preparation for making sharp turns, shifting the center of gravity backward quickly, and regaining the correct balance after transitions.

Here, the forehand of the horse turns around the inside hind leg in a half-circle (or later, in a full circle). The hind legs move at the rhythm of the walk. The inside hind leg moves on the spot, while the outside hind leg moves a hoof's length forward, and then sideways around the inside hind leg. At the same time, the forelegs are crossing each other in the sequence of the walk. The horse is bent around the rider's inside leg, and the rider looks in the direction of the turn. The rider sits to the inside, and with the inside rein leads the horse step by step around the inside hind leg, his outside rein controlling the degree of bending. The rider's inside leg prevents any backward deviation of the inside hind leg, while his outside leg moves the horse forward and around, thus preventing the horse from stepping back or to the outside.

The best way to prepare the horse for this movement is to make small circles, and then gradually diminish their size. It is important never to let the motion of the walk stop, nor to let the horse step backward. Avoid rushing this movement, and do not permit the horse to anticipate it. If it should start to do so, it is advisable to break up the turn with halts. Start one by one: forward one stride, sideways one stride, and halt. Then repeat again.

Half-Pass on Two Tracks

Performing the half-pass correctly is perhaps the most difficult exercise of the lateral movements. If the horse has learned correctly to perform leg-yielding, shoulder-in, and turns on the forehand and haunches, it will be well prepared to start learning this movement on two tracks. The best way to begin is to make a medium-sized half-circle at a walk and, when the horse is facing the opposite direction, make a shoulder-in to the inside. The rider should remain sitting inward, keeping the horse bent around his inside leg. The horse's forehand slightly precedes the hindquarters.

The rider's inside leg maintains the liveliness and preserves the horse's forward movement. His outside leg, through active lateral pressure, as-

Turn on the haunches: The hind legs are fairly well engaged, with the horse on the bit. The rider's position is correct, his weight more to the inside, the upper body slightly behind the vertical. The arms, elbows, and hand positions are all

correct. There is light contact with the horse's mouth, and its right shoulder is perfectly controlled. The draw rein is loose and is not in action. For jumpers, this execution is perfectly acceptable.

sures the lateral movement. The outside rein slightly holds back the horse's outside shoulder, which produces a lateral movement with the outside hind leg and foreleg crossing in front of the inside legs.

The degree of bending and the direction of the two tracks depends on the rider's coordinated aids being applied simultaneously, but with differing intensity.

In teaching the rider how to achieve the half-pass movement, the following procedure is recommended. The horse should already be bent slightly in the desired direction. The rider should establish an imaginary line on the ground from his inside seat bone and shoulder to the destination point toward which he wants to move on two tracks. If he tries to move his inside seat bone and hip along this imaginary line toward the desired point, he will use his aids correctly—instinctively—in striving to reach the desired point.

Always keep the front part of the horse leading. Its shoulders, neck, and head must always stay ahead of its hindquarters. Impulsion should not be lost, nor the gait hurried. Also, the half-pass should always be executed in a collected pace.

Once the exercise is being correctly performed at a walk, its execution at a trot and canter can be commenced, working in the same manner. Actually, the half-pass is easier to perform at a canter than in the walk or trot, but always bear in mind that the position at the canter must be straight; only the head should be slightly flexed.

In summary, the half-pass, together with the other lateral exercises, improves the obedience of the horse to the rider's aids, supples all parts of its body, and develops the engagement of its hindquarters.

Counter-Canter and Flying Change of Lead

The counter-canter is a superb schooling exercise, and every show jumper must learn to do it. It proves the suppleness of the horse and is a good exercise for the rider in coordinating his aids. It is also an effective method for straightening out the crookedness of the horse. And finally, the show jumper that is trained to counter-canter (or "false canter") will learn the flying change without difficulty.

Before it starts to learn the counter-canter, the horse must be well balanced and collected. When first attempting the counter-canter, it is wise to start cantering on a straight line and then proceed on a large half-circle in the opposite direction to that toward which the horse is bent. Then increase the tempo slightly, which will make it easier for the horse.

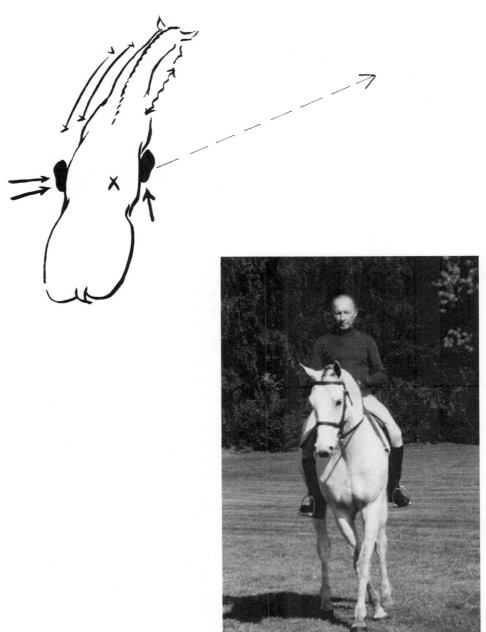

Two-track to the right (half-pass): The horse's outside forelegs cross in front of the inside leg. The horse is properly bent to the right and the right shoulder is leading slightly. The rider's weight is on his right seat bone; his outside (left) leg is somewhat behind the girth, actively supporting the side step of the outside hind leg. The rider's inside seat bone, hip, and shoulder move on the same imaginary line.

Most experts advise the rider not to change anything, i.e., to ride the counter-canter as he would the true canter, maintaining the same rhythm, keeping the same degree of bending, and maintaining the same seat. The rider's former inside leg remains the inside leg and continues, even more strongly, to support the impulsion of the strides; while the former outside leg remains the outside leg, actively encouraging the hind legs to follow the tracks of the forelegs. The outside rein leads the horse along and controls the outside shoulder. In other words, all the positions of the rider's legs and reins and their actions remain the same; the only exception is that the horse now canters in the opposite direction to its bending. It still follows the original leading shoulder and canters on a single track. From cantering on a straight line, the rider can easily execute the counter-canter by turning the opposite way to the horse's lead. The corner, however, must be well rounded at the beginning, and it is preferable to make several changes of rein across the diagonal, or ride large figure-eights, as well as serpentine lines, without changing the lead.

Show jumpers should be taught their flying change in long strides and not at a collected canter. It is easiest to perform the flying change when entering a corner on the false lead, or by riding a half-circle and changing rein when returning to the straight line again. Before attempting the flying change, a good preparation is to canter on one lead, then break the canter to a trot and pick up the other lead. By gradually reducing the number of trotting strides, one can eventually attempt the flying change in a corner or on a circle.

Let me now explain the rider's actions, supposing that he is cantering on the right rein. His inside leg maintains the canter, his inside rein leads the direction, and his outside rein maintains control of the horse's rhythm. His outside leg, slightly behind the girth, supports the hindquarters. Before giving the aid for the change, the horse's collection should be increased through a half-halt, and there must be strong support from the rider's legs to increase engagement of the hocks. Then follows an exact reversal of the positions of the rider's inside and outside legs, during the moment of suspension before the horse's new leading front leg touches the ground. At the same moment, the horse's head must be changed slightly to the inside, and the rider's weight shifted from the outside to the inside. All these changes must be made during the moment of suspension, and the horse must execute the change absolutely straight and forwardly; it should "jump" into the change.

Once the horse is doing good single flying changes on a straight line, it can be asked to do them every four or five strides. Attempting to train jumpers to do one- or two-tempo changes is unnecessary, however, and may even prove counterproductive, since repeated changes can sometimes be used as a defense during the horse's approach to a fence.

(Opposite) Riding two different horses in different places, the rider's classic style remains unchanged. His upper body position, contact, and leg positions are correct.

Neal Shapiro on Sloopy in Hickstead, England.

Neal Shapiro on Night Spree in London, White City, England, 1968.

7. Using Draw Reins and the Longe Line

It is not necessary to spend very much time at a horse show these days to realize how addicted riders have become to the use of draw reins and the longe line. From dawn on, horses by the dozen can be seen endlessly circling their "trainers" in an effort to "take the edge off them," while in the award of ribbons, half the horses if not more will enter the ring with their heads almost between their knees, held there by draw reins.

Both draw reins and longeing are of great value to the horseman—*if they are used intelligently and correctly*—but both can be, and often are abused through carelessness or ignorance. In this chapter I would like to set forth the methods that will enable draw reins and longeing to be used in the most effective, constructive ways.

Draw Reins

In general, most horses quickly learn to move forward in response to the rider's driving aids. In other words, the correct use of the driving seat and simultaneous driving leg aids in the appropriate place with appropriate intensity, will ordinarily produce forward movement. On a less sophisticated level, even a clumsy use of the whip and spurs will usually produce some kind of forward movement.

On the other hand, we must often face a serious problem with regard to the acceptance of our hands' influence and control. One of the primary reasons for this is that most horses start off on the forehand in the early stages of training. Inexperienced riders, not knowing how to engage the hindquarters enough, allow their horses to lean on their hands, seeking support. The more the horses succeed in this, the less sensitive their mouths become and the more they resist the rider's hand. (This is a common problem with horses from the racetrack.) One way to overcome this problem is for the rider to resist with his seat and back muscles (braced back) together with his arm and hand muscles, so that the horse cannot pull him out of the saddle. Of course, the rider's resistance must stop immediately when the horse eases the pull. This action and reaction of the rider must be applied repeatedly, even continuously.

The other way to succeed is through the proper use of draw reins. These are simply reins of approximately double length, that are fixed to the girth and run *through* the horse's bit ring and back to the rider's hand. Their invention is usually attributed to the Duke of Newcastle, but their proper use is thought to have been best developed by a famous Oberbereiter of the Spanish Riding School, Max von Weyrother, in the late nineteenth century.

The use of the draw rein—sometimes called Weyrother's running rein—will teach the horse to accept the hand and its controlling effect. The rider must be extremely skilled and experienced to use the draw rein properly. To fully understand the use of this special equipment, the way in which the draw rein functions must be analyzed. To begin, let me now explain the difference between the proper and improper use of the draw rein.

First, the problem of pulling is never the result of insensitivity of the horse's mouth. The problem lies with improper balance, by which is meant an inappropriate distribution of the rider's weight as well as that of the horse. When the horse is on the forehand, the forehand is overloaded; therefore, the horse seeks support, and leans on the hands of the rider. The real answer to pulling is thus to engage the hindquarters more, shifting the horse's center of gravity further backward.

When the horse pulls against the rider's hands and tries to lean on them for support, it is easier for the rider to resist that pull—still using a braced back and tightened muscles in his arms, hands, and legs—if he can employ the draw rein.

The draw rein should be fastened to the girth at a point higher than the point of the horse's shoulder. (In general, it should be horizontal to the ground, level with the horse's mouth.) After running through the snaffle ring, the rein goes back to the hands of the rider, which must be in their normal position, stabilized in front of the center of the rider's body and above the horse's withers. The rider's fingers are closed, and when the horse pulls forward, the hands tighten and do not give. The back muscles, along with the legs and hands, resist until the horse eases the pull; then all the muscles of the rider relax.

With a properly adjusted and utilized draw rein, the rider does *not* pull the horse's head behind the bit or down. The head of the horse is connected to its neck and back vertebrae through the first and second vertebrae. They are constructed to permit rotary-type movements of the head, as well as flexion and extension. Merely resisting the pull of the horse in his mouth does not bend these two vertebrae and will not result in getting the horse behind the bit. The signals of the hands are transmitted through the spinal cord and nerves to the hind legs.

Proper adjustment of the draw reins when inactive.

The draw reins in action, adjusted correctly.

The horse will learn sooner or later to accept the pressure of the bit in its mouth, and to understand the message of the hands telling it to slow down or turn, stop or rein back. We must keep in mind that all these results of influence are dependent upon adequate engagement of the hind-quarters.

It must be emphasized that the rider should never attempt to pull the head of the horse back or down, and will not do so by simply resisting the pull. Instead, the horse will learn to respect and accept the signals of the hands. The rider should *never* force the horse's head into position with the draw rein. This also explains why it is wrong to attach the draw rein to the girth between the front legs, for this only results in teaching the horse to get behind the bit, and enables it to *avoid* the control of the hand, and avoid engaging its hindquarters.

The application of the draw reins in this way will result in pulling apart the first *(atlas)* and second *(axis)* cervical vertebrae, which are constructed for flexion, not fixed as are the other five vertebrae. The horse will have to bend its head down, and will stay behind the bit as long as the rider maintains pressure on the draw reins. If the pressure ceases to exist, the horse will simply raise its head again, resuming the position it was in before, and continue to neglect the control of the hands.

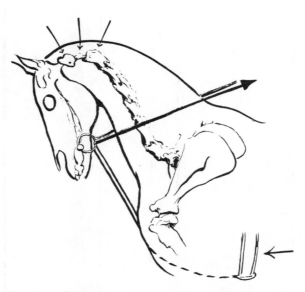

The incorrect application of the draw reins and its result. Note the bending of the axis and atlas.

The Horse on the Longe Line

Longeing—the training or exercise of a horse by having it move around its dismounted trainer at the end of a long "longe" line—is one of the most valuable tools the rider possesses. Though many riders think of it primarily as a form of light exercise or a means of wearing down a high-spirited horse before riding it, its greatest value, properly used, is for training. It looks easy, but it is not.

We all know that a correct seat on horseback and proper communication with the horse can be learned. Longeing the horse from the ground for various purposes must be learned just as carefully, for it is an art that takes long experience to master. Regretfully, this is not always recognized; yet much damage can be done to the horse, physically as well as mentally, by using the longe line without the requisite understanding, knowledge, and experience—not to mention patience.

Longeing the horse is not very different from actual riding, but carrying it out correctly, so that the desired results are obtained, is perhaps even more difficult than riding. Since working the horse on the longe is an important part of the horse's fundamental education and training, we will discuss it in some detail, dealing both with how to do it, and why.

The horse ready for longeing.

The longe line is in the trainer's outside hand, and the whip is under his inside arm, behind his body.

Thanks to the instinct of self-preservation that most horses possess, as well as their common sense, the horse will quite often compensate for an inexperienced rider's mistakes, and usually recovers quickly from a bad incident. Unfortunately, this is not always the case when the horse is on the longe line; here, an untrained person can easily hurt the horse physically and interfere with its natural instinct, or confuse it mentally and ruin the animal's confidence for a long time.

The basic principles for longeing the horse are just the same as for riding. Longeing does *not* just mean making the horse run around in a circle.

The trainer's position in relation to the horse, and the presence of his long longeing whip create the forwardness, while the contact through the longe line works to direct and control, just as do the reins in the rider's hands.

The position of the trainer should remain in the center of the circle on which the longed horse travels. Ideally the trainer remains in the same spot and turns on his own center, step by small step, always keeping his right leg advanced when the horse is on the left rein, and vice versa. (This position aids the trainer's balance in case of a sudden unexpected action by the horse.) However, this center-of-the-circle position of the trainer will only be possible when the horse is fully trained and thoroughly accustomed to the longe line; for it requires the horse to be attentive, and complete control and confidence to have been established.

Until the horse arrives at that degree of training—as in the case of young horses—the trainer's position must be more flexible, and always somewhat *behind* the horse. This position gives the horse the feeling that the area in front of him is open, that the "door is open," encouraging him to move forward. As the trainer places himself more nearly in line with the shoulder of the horse, or even moves slightly ahead of the shoulder, the horse tends to decrease its speed, for the "door is closing." If the trainer shortens the longe line and moves closer to the horse, he will inhibit the tendency of the horse to cut inside the circle. It is rarely appropriate for the trainer to move even slightly ahead of the horse. His movements in assuming and retaining the correct position must be quick, but always smoothly controlled if he is to avoid frightening or confusing the horse. He must always watch the eye of the horse to be able to respond instantly to an unexpected movement. He must, in fact, be virtually obsessed with the horse, and should never let his attention wander away to anything but the horse.

It is a good idea never to longe a young horse in an open field. The corner of an arena or a longeing ring is the proper place, and the circle should be as large as possible. The young horse should learn to respond to the trainer's voice and acquire confidence in the longe whip, rather than

The trainer's position longeing the horse over cavalletti: (Above) Trainer is as much behind the horse as its impulsion and willingness to move forward require. (Below) Proper longe-line and whip positions.

become afraid of it. Quite a long time must be spent at the walk and trot on the longe line. At the beginning, the canter will be too difficult for the young horse on the circle; it will not be able to keep its balance and rhythm coordinated, and will tend to become disunited, crossing its legs behind and easily getting on the forehand.

The longe line should be held in organized equal loops in the outside hand of the trainer before it is attached to the cavesson rings or the bit.

The cavesson was invented hundreds of years ago and should be used for longeing young horses because it does not harm their mouth. (Older horses can be longed on a regular snaffle bridle, with the reins tied up so that they do not flap around, and preferably combined with the use of side reins.) The padded iron part of the cavesson must be buckled snugly on the horse's nose, and the straps on the outside of the face must be checked to insure that they are not too close to the horse's eyes. Though regular use of the side reins is not a must, they are advisable, and will be dealt with later on. The side reins should be fastened to the girth and the snaffle rings, or to the outside rings of the cavesson's noseband.

It is not unusual for the young horse to attempt to run away from the trainer. Therefore, all four ankles should be protected by some type of boot to protect against physical damage.

Steady, light contact with the horse's mouth must be maintained with the longe line. The horse must be longed in both directions, changing reins and gaits. It should learn the signals for transitions and must also learn to halt and stand still.

After the longe line is attached to the bit or cavesson, the trainer slips the line's end loop around his wrist (left wrist if the horse is moving to the left, and vice versa) and holds the other loops around the same hand, to permit give-and-take of the line and make it secure. One should never let any part of the line drop to the ground. The trainer establishes light contact with the mouth or nose of the horse and moves the horse forward. To maintain contact, he makes the necessary adjustments either by shortening or lengthening the line, or moving his hand closer to or further away from his body.

The trainer must hold the hand with the longe line in front of his outer shoulder at the level of the horse's mouth. His upper body should be parallel to the point of the horse's shoulder, and the longe whip held in his inside hand, pointed toward the horse's hock.

There is a more sophisticated way of connecting the longe line for the contact, which is more effective and offers more control than using the cavesson, but should be used only for older horses and by more experienced hands; otherwise, it can be most harmful. It is called the "Continental Way" (though it is actually the Germans who are credited with its invention). In the Continental Way, the end of the longe rein is run through the near-side ring of the bit, behind the ears and over the poll of the horse, and snapped or buckled to the off-side ring. A correctly adjusted regular side rein may also be used, as with the cavesson.

As we have said, the longe line serves the same role as the rein in the hands of the rider. The longe whip, pointed toward the inside hock, follows the horse's hock from behind and supports its rhythm and impulsion. If necessary, it quietly and rhythmically moves up and down toward the hock, thus representing the rider's forward-driving leg.

The trainer's position, his steady light contact with the mouth of the horse, and the uninterrupted support of the forward-driving whip must all be coordinated so that they act together simultaneously.

There are several reasons for working the horse on the longe line, and it is important to explain them separately. Putting the horse on the longe line is ideal preparatory work for a young horse before breaking it to the rider. Later on the horseback training will be much easier, for the young horse by then will be familiar with and have acquired confidence in his trainers. The longe line is also an excellent introduction to basic discipline; the horse learns to walk and trot around without fear, and even learns to halt and stand still. It becomes accustomed to the trainer's voice and to the longe whip. It is thus not disturbed by the weight of the rider, and learns to relax while gradually strengthening its muscles.

Extremely calm handling is necessary during longeing, and any fight must be carefully avoided.

For preparatory work with young horses, a properly adjusted, well-padded cavesson should be used over a snaffle bridle, and snugly adjusted on the nose bone. A surcingle should be buckled over the saddle, and side reins should be attached to it and to the bridle ring of the bit. Side reins are helpful because the horse should be in a "frame" from the very beginning of training.

For the young horse, the side reins should be adjusted with a very moderate, even tension on both sides, rather than hanging loose with almost no contact. If the horse tries to run away without side reins, the trainer can only pull on its head and neck, and will have no control at all over the outside shoulder. This creates a situation in which the front and hind ankles can cross and hit each other and serious damage can occur.

The use of an assistant in starting to longe a young horse is very helpful. If the horse tries to run away or turns in the opposite direction, the helper can then lead the young, excited horse back to the correct track and calm it down, which is always the clever thing to do.

It is very useful to jump young horses at a trot on the longe line. The fences must be specially set up for longeing, always starting low; poles should be placed alongside the fences to act as wings—to guide the young horse and prevent his cutting in or by-passing the fence. The contact with

the longe line must be light, sensitively following the movement and not interfering with the horse's mouth. The horse has to figure out for himself the proper take-off distance, and should fall back to a trot almost immediately after the landing. This work, when done well, is very relaxing and gives the young horse confidence to jump, without rushing. Later, little oxers and even higher fences can be used, but they should be introduced, of course, only gradually.

Another important use for longeing the horse is to educate and train it. The horse's balance can be improved, and its rhythm effectively regulated by using the voice and vibrating the longe whip so that the tempo is decreased and the strides thus lengthened. Transitions can also be taught. If the more advanced horse is drawn onto a smaller circle, maintaining the same impulsion will automatically produce more collection and more longitudinal bending of the body. This exercise should only be requested for a short period of time, and followed by driving the horse out onto a large circle and extending its stride.

Whenever the horse is being longed without a rider, side reins should always be used. However, if we are retraining a spoiled older horse, especially to accept the action of the hands, then the use of draw reins is even more effective than side reins. In this case, however, the trainer must be very experienced.

For this sort of work the draw reins are fixed under the stirrup leathers and tied behind the pommel of the saddle with a knot, as shown in the illustration. The principles involved are the same as if the draw reins were in the hands of a rider. The only difference is that in longeing, the ends of the draw reins are not held by the rider.

The adjustment must be made as follows: Place the horse on a level surface, standing evenly on its four legs with its head and neck held in a natural position. Take both sides of the draw reins together in one hand and hold them above the pommel, making only the lightest contact with the horse's mouth, and make a knot there. The draw reins should be fixed with one loop around the top of the stirrup leathers on both sides. This creates a triangle; the draw rein, attached to the girth, passes through the snaffle's ring and goes back to the knot behind the pommel. If the horse does not pull its head forward or try to stretch its neck, there is no pressure in its mouth. If the horse *does* pull, or tries to go above the bit, the triangle will not give, and pressure occurs until it gives up the pull, relaxes, and returns its head to the natural position. Sooner or later this experience becomes convincing and the horse learns to respect the pressure in its mouth. By using the draw rein in this way, the head of the horse is not forced down into position, but the horse itself finds the right position in which to carry its head: the natural position.

(Opposite) A young horse jumps on the longe line: (Top) A perfect take-off point. (Center) Over the jump—correct bascule. (Bottom) Landing—longe-line contact is correct. The elastic side lines are used in light contact.

The end of the draw rein that is attached to the girth should never be fastened below the level of the point of the shoulder. Using the draw rein in this fashion, with the longe line adjusted in the Continental Way as described earlier, is potentially severe, and in inexperienced hands can be more dangerous than a razor in the hands of a monkey. With a skilled trainer, however, the results can be remarkable.

By repeating the half-bending to the inside that occurs automatically on the longe line, and with continued forward driving, maintaining good impulsion, the horse will soon find the bit itself with a correct neck and head position, and thus learn to carry itself on the bit. The beneficial result of such longeing is obvious: The horse remains on the same circular track in all gaits, keeping the same rhythm, by itself, moving evenly and keeping its attention focused on the trainer. The fixed draw-rein contact is light, elastic, and vibrating—teaching the horse that it is more pleasant not to pull, and not to fight. When the horse's neck is naturally arched and its head is in front of the vertical line, the trainer can maintain contact with two fingers and follow the horse's hock with the longe whip quietly, almost without any interference. In this frame, the horse is composed, well balanced both physically and mentally, in consistent contact with the bit, and both lively and suppled.

Attaching the draw rein: From the saddle, the draw rein is run through the ring of the bit, then to the top of the pommel, and is fixed under the stirrup leather. The longe line goes through the inside ring of the bit, over the poll of the horse, and is fixed to the outside ring of the bit.

Seat Improvement Through Longeing

There is no better way to establish a correct seat—the foundation of all riding—than by riding on the longe without stirrups. Such practice makes sense only if the horse is well trained on the longe line; it must have a good disposition and move evenly and calmly, so that the instructor and rider may both concentrate on the details of the rider's seat. Both rider and instructor must be able to analyze where the difficulties lie, and find appropriate exercises to help overcome any special problems.

There are, of course, general exercises which are useful for everyone. Their aim is to develop a strong seat, thus making it possible for the rider to use his leg and hand aids independently as well as simultaneously, and to obtain the right feeling of coordination.

Side reins should be used for the horse so that the instructor can control the horse and the rider can perform all the required movements with his body without touching the reins. It is important to emphasize that the rider should make continuous seat corrections every time he feels that he has lost the rhythm or the right contact with the back of the horse, or feels that he is starting to squeeze his thighs to keep himself in the saddle. In pulling himself back into the saddle, the rider should grasp the pommel with his *outside* hand, and the cantle with his *inside* hand, for this is the only effective way to make these corrections. If the correction is made in this way, the rider's outside shoulder remains in a forward position and his inside seat bone sinks deeper into the saddle, along with the inside hip. Soon the rider finds his seat again and picks up the horse's rhythm; he can then relax and stay soft in his body when the exercises are resumed.

Periodic seat correction on the longe line is equally necessary for advanced riders, for everyone falls into bad habits sometimes, especially during concentrated training sessions, and even more so during continuous competition. Though checking oneself in a mirror can be of great help, it is difficult to analyze oneself objectively, and every rider will benefit from being observed, critiqued, and corrected by someone knowledgeable on the ground. Riding without stirrups, except when on the longe line, will not usually serve as an adequate method of seat correction. What usually happens instead is that the rider, being less secure in the saddle, simply relies upon the reins—in fact, on the mouth of the horse—for support. Consequently, instead of correcting his seat, he begins to hang in the horse's mouth, pinching its sides and gradually losing the proper place to sit altogether.

Of course, riders of the highest level of expertise, such as the riders of the Spanish Riding School, are able to use their firmly established seats

(Top) Rider's seat correction on the longe line: The outside hand is on the pommel, the inside hand is behind the saddle from the front.

Three exercises on the longe line: (Opposite, bottom) Upper body turns to the right and left; (top) rider rotates upper body without changing the position of the hips; (bottom) rider reaches up with hand and makes circles with them.

Young horse over cavalletti with elastic side reins: (Top) The horse is stretching down while the trainer is close behind, his whip following the hocks. (Bottom) The trainer follows closely with light longe-line contact. (Opposite, top) The trainer's whip is in the perfect position, directly behind the horse's hocks. The

footprints are exactly in the middle of the cavalletti. (Bottom) The trainer gives the horse more freedom, lengthens the longe line, and stays more behind as the young horse begins to show confidence.

without stirrups very effectively, but in general, this practice is not recommended for less advanced riders.

Just as the normal proper seat can be developed or corrected by putting the rider on a longe line without stirrups, so too can the jumping seat be stabilized and improved. Since the rider has nothing to do with the management of the horse itself, which remains under the control of the trainer, he is able to concentrate on what every part of his body is doing over the jump. Experiencing the right feeling at take-off and landing, the stable support of weight on the knees and the steady position of the legs, as well as the independent hands, are all goals that can be achieved while jumping low fences on the longe line without stirrups.

Older horses can be exercised on the longe line to loosen up their muscles without having to carry a rider's weight, and it is also a good idea to longe any horse after a demanding performance, such as lots of jumping or a cross-country competition; longeing is a much better refresher than leaving the horse in the stable box. A saddle or surcingle with side reins and leg protection is mandatory in these cases, and a sufficiently experienced person should always do the longeing if the trainer or rider is not available.

Cavalletti work can also be introduced to the horse on the longe line, using the equipment described above. For younger horses, use side lines; for older horses (or retraining spoiled horses) it is better to use draw reins, as previously discussed.

8. The Origins of Cavalletti Training

Though the basic principles of riding and training were first discussed by Xenophon, and elaborated in ever increasing detail through the centuries, there is very little literature on the training and riding of jumpers until the late nineteenth century. The reason is simple: Until the English Enclosure Acts of the eighteenth century, which made it necessary for a fox hunter to jump in order to stay with his hounds, there simply were not many fences in the countryside, nor much reason to jump them.

By the mid-nineteenth century, however, hunting to hounds over enclosed agricultural land was common both in the British Isles and on the Continent, and the steeple-chasing and then show jumping that followed it were increasingly popular with the public. We can get a good idea of the style of riding that was used at that time by examining the prints and paintings of the hunts and steeple-chases of the period. The rider's upper body was held in a vertical position, the rider sitting rather far back, with long, straight legs and very long stirrups. To maintain their balance while jumping, riders leaned back, letting their legs move forward, and slipped their reins, so that they had to gather them up again upon landing.

This was the style of riding and jumping that was taught in the cavalry schools of Europe, sometimes with the added variation of "lifting" the horse off the ground by its mouth, a technique that obviously made it virtually impossible for the horse to use its head and neck in order to balance itself. Jumping in that fashion must have been a very unpleasant experience for the horse!

Even so, some big fences were jumped in that way—high-jump classes were being won at over seven feet well before the turn of the century; but nothing seems more obvious today than that the horse's basic jumping mechanism is the *bascule*—using its two ends in a counterbalanced way, like a seesaw—and that anything inhibiting this mechanism works to the detriment of the horse's natural instinct and capacity to jump.

Federico Caprilli (1868–1907), an Italian cavalry officer, must be credited with changing the old military concept of lifting the horse's forelegs off the ground with its mouth and leaning back in the air. He envisioned riders following the horse's movement in the air instead of moving backward in contrary motion to it, thus enabling the horse to use its head and neck freely as a counterbalance. He realized that to apply this revolutionary concept, the rider's position at take-off would have to change: He would have to shift his center of gravity forward, sensitively following the horse's mouth with his hand, and thus require shorter stirrups. This firmer leg position in turn assured more support for the rider's upper body, and it became easier for him to follow the horse's bascule.

In retrospect, Caprilli's theory was basically simple, but it took some time for others to realize and accept its practicality. He kept working at the "natural method," as he called it, for he believed in long years of practice. It took almost five years for his method to become accepted, during which time he suffered many accidents while experimenting (partly due, perhaps, to his own elongated trunk and relatively short legs).

Nevertheless, Caprilli's system spread, and gradually it became generally adopted and employed throughout the world. Caprilli died from injuries incurred in a riding accident at the early age of thirty-nine, and sadly, only a few written notes of his ideas were ever found. But the fundamental logic of his methodology remains, and his concepts have since dominated the entire equestrian world.

Caprilli believed firmly in the basic training of the horse. He felt that the horse must be disciplined and obedient, not so much through constant drilling, but by employing a more natural approach. The horse should use his own system to keep his natural balance once he is carrying the added weight of the rider, and the rider's adjustment to that was Caprilli's concept. He knew the horse could also jump as a result of fear, throwing itself over the jump, but he believed that this was usually the result of its fear of the rider. Caprilli deviated from the unnatural, military foundation of equitation, and that is his great and everlasting contribution to our equestrian sport.

His system was uncomplicated: Change the rider's position; do not disturb the horse's natural balance; train the horse to take care of itself and yet be disciplined, obedient, and confident in its rider.

Caprilli was convinced that logical and systematic training was necessary for the jumper. His training area was a country field, and his program involved jumping many low fences from a trot, and trotting over rails on the ground. Eventually he added little feet to the rails to stabilize and slightly raise them, so that they resembled little saw horses, or *cavalletti*. He believed in making many transitions in order to achieve discipline. He also believed in quiet work, trying to "show the ground to the horse," i.e., show the horse where it is about to put its feet. He based his exercises on logical principles and asked nothing artificial or unnatural of the horse.

Rider's position over the jump, mid-nineteenth century.

Joe Fargis on Bonte II in Wolfsburg, Germany, 1971. The strong knee and leg position allows flexibility for the upper body and hands.

Carol Hoffman on Trick Track in Wiesbaden, Germany, 1966. The nice bascules of the horse reflect the rider's proper style and influence.

For him, it was essential to build up the horse's confidence that the rider would never harm it. He believed that a good jumper does not have to be "helped" during the jump, but should be left undisturbed. He advocated keeping the hands as low as possible at the sides of the horse's withers. Only in certain situations would he use exercises without stirrups, and even then would do so only in moderation, to avoid stiffness in the rider. As far as jumping was concerned, he was mostly interested in developing the horse's ability to find the right take-off point by itself. He felt that this ability was partly a natural instinct, and partly acquired through long practice over low obstacles approached in a trot.

With the adoption of Caprilli's system, systematic instruction in jumping began. To introduce his method, Caprilli placed poles on the ground, three to four feet apart, and made the horse walk over them in both directions. Then he placed the poles four feet or more apart and let the horse trot over them quietly. The number of poles was gradually increased, and the distances in between were widened to five feet. This marked the beginning of the systematic use of cavalletti.

Originally the cavalletti were used by Caprilli and his followers in a very simple way. Walking and trotting over the poles on the ground helped the horses to relax; they learned to cooperate with their riders, as the riders got a chance to practice the newly invented riding position.

Next the poles were raised a little higher (one and a half feet) and placed in a row, twelve to fifteen feet apart. Horses cantered over these low cavalletti without taking a stride in between, and learned to stretch their necks and take care of themselves. The rider was supposed to not interfere with the horse's mouth, but to concentrate only on his forward position, balancing on his knees and supporting himself with strong legs on the sides of the horse, thus stabilizing his upper body. This new method proved quite effective; the riders improved greatly and realized how much better and more happily their horses jumped. The riders got a safer feeling over the obstacles as well.

The Caprilli concept was adopted by most army cavalry schools in Europe shortly after 1900, and many nations developed training facilities modeled after the Italian Pinerolo Riding School. Open ditches, post-and-rail fences, and walls with poles were permanently built in a row at the correct distances with one or two strides in between, and all were jumped at a comfortable, lively canter.

The different cavalry schools employed Caprilli's *sistema* in slightly different ways, depending upon the rest of their curriculum; Germany, for example, combined it with their own dressage training, and this combination was responsible for the great German jumping teams before World War II. I myself was exposed to both the Hungarian and German adaptations of Caprilli as a young cavalry officer and instructor before the war, and can attest that the basic elements of his method were followed very faithfully. We used both the trotting poles and the jumping grids, and sometimes used a small placing fence before a larger one in order to control the take-off. However, we were not taught to use the cavalletti and the grid together, the method I now favor. In the next chapter I will describe in detail how to do so, and how to vary these ingredients in such a way that they can help solve almost any training problem.

9. A Modern Cavalletti System

I was engaged as coach of the U.S. Equestrian Team jumping squad in the spring of 1955, shortly after the team returned from the Pan American Games in Mexico City. I was asked to help the team prepare for a European tour that summer, and to accompany it; this would start the team's preparation for the 1956 Olympic Games, to be held in Stockholm.

There was not much time before the team left for Europe, and it was obvious that I could not possibly attempt to change the horses and riders in drastic ways; I had to figure out methods which would let them build on what they already knew, while gradually developing techniques that would help them cope with European competitive conditions, which were very different from those they were familiar with from domestic competition. I concluded that if I could find a way to control the horses' take-off without upsetting their temperaments, I could enable both the horses and riders to practice what they needed to work on. The system of cavalletti to control the take-off, combined with gymnastics—as described in this chapter and the next—produced exactly the desired result.

The method of using cavalletti and gymnastics that I devised and developed through necessity is a very flexible one, and does not need to be applied according to rigid, hard and fast rules. Yet if it is employed intelligently and imaginatively, it can help to solve many different problems, and can almost infallibly help to develop whatever potential ability both the horses and the riders possess, in a shorter period of time than might otherwise be required.

Let me start by describing the proper equipment, the construction of which should be both simple and practical. The most suitable poles are round and quite heavy, about six inches in diameter, six feet long, and stabilized at both ends by a foot-long base. Two of these together make a twelve-foot pole, which is just comfortable to work with. Each piece should be heavy enough not to move out of position every time the horse's hoof hits it, and yet not so heavy that one person cannot easily carry or replace it.

Another type of construction that is often seen employs crossed feet, like the letter X, to support the poles. This type of cavalletti can be very dangerous, for if the horse stumbles over the cavalletti, the rider may fall with his back or head landing right on top of the crossed feet.

In the absence of specially constructed cavalletti poles, single poles on the ground can be used, with a little dirt pushed up on both sides to prevent the pole from rolling when the horse merely grazes it. Even if supported, the poles should not be higher than six or eight inches from the ground.

The correct distances between the cavalletti poles are most important for the proper use of this method, otherwise the horse can easily become confused. The principle here is to never interfere with the natural rhythm and length of stride of the particular horse we are working with, which, unfortunately, makes it awkward to work over cavalletti with several different horses at the same time. The distances usually need some adjustment—sometimes just a couple of inches—to suit each individual horse, allowing for their differences in size, age, disposition, and level of training.

The normal distances between vary from 4 to 5 feet. Horses of average age, size, and experience can usually start with 4 feet, 6 inch to 4 feet, 9 inch distances. However, after a couple of tries one can observe if some adjustment is necessary, one way or the other, and the spacing can be adjusted to the natural length of the particular horse's stride. Later, in advanced training, when the horse's stride has been established through the cavalletti work, we can develop more collected or extended gaits by gradually shortening or lengthening the distances between the poles.

For mental preparation of the horses, it is good to start by scattering single poles on the ground without any particular spacing in between, in different positions and different directions, and then walking over them on loose reins. This serves to relax the horse and develop its confidence. This work can then be continued at a trot with lots of variations and transitions, and then we can start placing the cavalletti in a row.

Four cavalletti in a row are just the right eventual number for our purposes, but these should be introduced to the horse gradually. We should start with one cavalletti, and walk and trot over it until the horse has become familiar with the idea of stepping over it, and does not try to jump it.

Adding only a second cavalletti often does not work out well; the horse will try to jump the two poles together, instead of stepping over them one after the other. It is preferable to add two or three cavalletti instead, which eliminates the possibility of the horse jumping over them all together; gradually it will figure out what to do, if we keep our patience.

What is the benefit to the horse of trotting over cavalletti? Our primary goal is to capture the horse's attention and focus its concentration on the ground. It is an old horse master's axiom: "Show your horse the ground." Trotting over the cavalletti encourages the horse to stretch its neck down from the shoulder and look where to put its feet. Because it must lift its feet higher over the poles than it would on flat ground, its tendons and muscles—especially those of the hindquarters—become stronger. Furthermore, in concentrating on the ground and stretching its neck, the horse raises its spine and surrounding muscles, thus loosening up its back. In short, the entire musculature of the horse becomes conditioned and relaxed.

The horse will adjust its rhythm almost instinctively to the cavalletti distances, if they are accurate, as it concentrates on avoiding the poles. It will stabilize its rhythm itself and relax. Its length of stride will also be regulated if there is no change in impulsion. The fore- and hind feet should step exactly halfway between the poles. Thus, if the horse's rhythm and impulsion increase, its strides will lengthen and its hoofprints

Use of the cavalletti: Bertalan de Némethy on San Lucas in Aachen, Germany, 1972. The horse's legs are in perfect coordination. The hoofprints are in the middle of the poles. The rider's position is correct.

Conrad Homfeld on Triple Crown in Hamburg, Germany, 1971. This picture exhibits perfect harmony; elbows are well down, though the hands could be a little lower.

will come closer and closer to each successive pole. This usually happens when the rider's influence disturbs the horse or the distances between the cavalletti are too short. If the distances are too long, the horse will not be able to lengthen its strides sufficiently and will try to put another short stride between, or try to jump over it. Needless to say, either result is the opposite of what we want to achieve.

When the cavalletti work is carried out carefully and knowingly, the horse's balance improves tremendously, as does the control and coordination of its whole body. It will both develop confidence in itself mentally and benefit physically, becoming more regulated, harmonious, flexible, and relaxed. It will learn to shift its center of gravity quickly and surely. All these components will fall into place and develop a sound foundation for jumping.

How does the rider benefit from training over cavalletti? Jumping obstacles skillfully and safely depends primarily upon taking off at the right point. The rider's ability to "see" this desirable take-off point—what we call "timing" or "having a good eye"—can be developed or improved upon by the use of cavalletti. The essence of timing is being able to translate into strides the visual distance to the fence from as far away as possible,

William (Buddy) Brown on Sandsablaze in Aachen, Germany, 1976. Upper body and contact are correct but legs are a little behind.

Dennis Murphy on Commodore in Aachen, Germany, 1978. Classic style in every respect.

Rider's timing through use of cavalletti: Note the confident approach, with no change in rhythm. As the horse proceeds through the cavalletti, the rider maintains correct rein contact, and a straight line from her elbow to the horse's bit.

while at the same time sensing how much impulsion it will take to get there.

When jumping lower fences, especially single fences, the right striding can often be taken care of by a balanced horse with a good temperament. Horses seem to have a sixth sense when it comes to judging the point from which they will have to take off. Such is not the case, however, with bigger fences and combinations; here the rider must learn when to remain passive and when to intervene. He can only increase or decrease the horse's impulsion in accordance with his own sense of timing or "eye"; in other words, he must decide whether to lengthen or shorten the horse's stride in order to reach the ideal take-off point.

While trotting over the cavalletti, the rider automatically practices his timing. Approaching the first cavalletti pole, he must realize where he is at least six strides before, and he must use his judgment immediately and instinctively so as not to get too close or too far.

The horse should step over the first cavalletti without having to alter its impulsion or length of stride at all. As it continues over the rest of the cavalletti, the rider must regulate its impulsion just as he will between obstacles later during competition. Failing to do so will confuse the horse, which will then have to scramble through. Practice over cavalletti will also give the rider a feeling of unity with his horse and develop his coordination both with its center of gravity and its movements. The rider's position will become more secure and balanced, since his position is stabilized from the hip down to the heels, and strongly supported on the knees; and his hands will become more independent, enabling him to perfect an elastic contact with the horse's mouth.

It is better to use a posting trot for cavalletti work than a sitting trot, and there are several good reasons for this. In the posting trot, the rider has a better feeling for the rhythm of the horse, and can more easily avoid interfering with the horse's movement or its mouth. Very few riders are capable of not disturbing the horse's back and mouth while sitting to the trot. Using a posting trot, the rider can also dictate the rhythm for the horse more easily, as we have explained earlier.

The rider should concentrate first on making a correct approach to the first cavalletti, neither reaching with the stride nor making an extra short stride. Continuously controlling the horse's impulsion, the rider can dictate its rhythm by letting one diagonal pair of legs throw his seat forward in the posting movement, and then, as the diagonal's hind leg touches the ground, lowering his seat back into the saddle in perfect harmony with this movement. This physical action of the rider—moving his seat forward close to the saddle in the direction of the pommel, and dropping the seat softly down into the saddle—must be executed rhythmically and energetically. As a result, the horse will respond and adjust itself to this rhythmical impulse.

It is desirable, before commencing exercises over the cavalletti, to always include preparation using the elementary training movements. Cavalletti work should never be started before the horse has been put on the bit through transitions and bending exercises with many changes of direction. The secret to proper preparation is not so much the length of time spent, as the lively alternation of several different training movements. The horse thus never becomes bored with endless drills; its interest and willingness remain alive.

Using Cavalletti to Control the Take-off

There are many advantages in cavalletti training in addition to those already discussed. They can enable us to improve the jumping technique of the horse by using a controlled take-off point, as they help the rider improve his style over the fence; at the same time, they also afford the instructor the opportunity to observe the horse and rider in what amounts to slow motion. In any sport, better results can be achieved with better style, and so it is in riding and jumping. A correct style can be learned and must be practiced, while always remembering that good style in jumping depends upon the center of gravity of the horse in motion, which in turn is controlled by physical laws.

The take-off point is that spot in front of the obstacle from which the horse leaves the ground in order to jump the fence. The distance of this point from the obstacle is not always the same; it varies depending upon the height and spread of the fence, as well as its type of construction. The take-off point also depends upon the horse's speed, its length of stride, and its basic jumping mechanism.

All these different factors must be taken into consideration during training, and only practice will help develop the sense of knowing where the right take-off position should be. Each different circumstance, as well as the rider's timing, will have some influence on the position of the correct take-off point.

Since we can control the horse's impulsion and speed by using four correctly spaced cavalletti, we can also control the correct take-off point for a fence (crossed rails) built after the cavalletti. This fence should be placed nine to ten feet beyond the last cavalletti—twice the distance between any two cavalletti themselves. By controlling the take-off in this way, it will be stabilized and can be practiced over and over, so that the jumping technique of the horse as well as the style of the rider can be corrected and developed.

Let us examine what actually happens. Aside from all the other benefits, using the cavalletti for practicing the take-off and jumping technique also saves the horse physically. The height and spread of the crossed poles, or

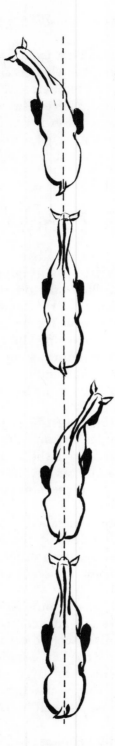

Preparation exercise before using cavalletti—loosening the horse's back and loin by changing its bending to both sides.

the parallel poles used later, need never be too great, since the horse's impulsion is controlled through the cavalletti. Training over single fences without the cavalletti might easily lead to more and bigger fences, requiring much more effort from the horse, and thus wearing it out much more quickly. The rider approaches the four cavalletti at a posting trot. As the horse advances over the last cavalletti with one pair of diagonal legs, and the rider lowers his seat into the saddle as that hind leg touches down, the horse's leading foreleg thrusts off, since there is no room in which to make another stride. The other diagonal hind leg follows this action, and moves alongside the first hind leg. Both hocks bend and receive the backward shift of the center of gravity, and the hindquarters lift the whole body up and over.

The two hind hoofprints will be seen at about a five- to six-foot distance from the cross-pole fence. The most sensitive moment for the horse occurs as it attempts the effort of lifting the weight of its own body plus its rider's into the air. At this moment the rider must be in the right position and must not disturb the horse's balance nor anticipate the jump with his upper-body movement. When he feels that the second hind leg has moved over the last cavalletti and is placed close to the other one, the rider's seat settles into the saddle and waits for the elevation of the horse's forehand, initiated by the thrust of the leading foreleg. The rider's upper body bends quietly forward, folding mostly at the hip joints. The amount of folding depends on the size of the fence, but the rider must always avoid pushing his center of gravity ahead of that of the horse. In other words, the rider should never throw his upper body ahead of the horse's center of gravity, for if he should do so, the horse will speed up its jump, which will interfere with its basculing technique, and force it to get flat over the fence.

If the rider anticipates at the take-off point, it disturbs the horse's balance and concentration almost as badly as if he is "left behind." Being left behind does not happen very often, and usually only with rank beginners. On the other hand, a great many riders tend to get ahead of the horse over the jump. If the take-off point is controlled by the cavalletti the rider can learn to overcome this bad habit as well as improve his horse's jumping technique.

It is natural for the horse in jumping to stretch out its neck and head to counterbalance its hindquarters; this forms a curved body shape which aids the mechanism of the bascule. The horse's bascule can be very much improved upon by using a controlled take-off point following the cavalletti. By gradually raising and widening a fence of parallel poles placed about nine to ten feet behind the last cavalletti, the horse's hindquarters must create more power to push higher and stretch its body more widely over the fence. As a result, it must make more effort to stay round, and it will use its bascule extensively.

Ellen Raidt Lordi on Morven in Farmington, Connecticut, 1979. The proper, classical position over the fence.

Joe Fargis on Bonte in Fontainebleau, 1971, displays the most classic position of the upper body and legs.

Hugh Wiley on Master William in London, White City, England, 1959.

Hugh Wiley on Nautical in Wiesbaden, Germany, 1959.

In these pictures the rider's rein contact with each of the horses over the fence is perfect. His upper body follows the impulsion of the horse.

Rider's position from before the take-off to the landing: (Top) Take-off point approached from the cavalletti. The left diagonal is moving over the last cavalletti. (Bottom) The right foreleg thrusts off; the two hind legs are close together and engage to lift the body. The rider's body is slightly forward but does not anticipate. Her hands maintain the contact and remain low on the sides of the neck.

(Top) The rider's upper body and her contact with the horse's mouth are perfect. There is an unbroken straight line from her elbow to the horse's mouth. The legs are in the correct position. (Bottom) Before landing, the rider is still in a forward position, but her seat bones are close to the saddle. Her weight is on her knees and her hands are correct, maintaining light contact.

Experience has shown that a horse with above-average jumping ability can readily jump from a trot four-foot parallel poles or even higher ones. Not only does the horse's technique improve, but its self-confidence also increases and it realizes, as does its rider, that increased speed is not necessarily essential to jumping bigger fences.

These advantages are obtained only if the rider is able not to disturb the horse's balance or his harmonious relationship with the horse, and can smoothly follow the horse's mouth with his hands. When the forehand of the horse starts to rise, the rider starts to quietly lean forward with his upper body, and his weight leaves the back of the horse, though his seat bones should still remain very close to the saddle. More weight is shifted onto his knees, while the lower legs' contact with the sides of the horse becomes tighter and prevents them from shifting either forward or backward. It is important for the rider *not* to push the seat out of the saddle. This would result in losing contact with the body of the horse, since the rider will put more weight on the stirrups in order to support his upper body, and less weight will be placed on the thighs and knees, leaving the upper body to be supported by the mouth of the horse.

In the correct position, the rider remains close to the horse's body from his seat bones down to his heels. Since it so closely follows the horse's center of gravity, the rider's weight becomes almost part of the horse's own body. This gives the horse a feeling of security when it moves or jumps. The rider's upper body movement should never be exaggerated. The less the rider's body moves above the horse's body, the better.

The rider's elastic contact with the horse's mouth remains the same over the fence; the hands are kept quite low on either side of the horse's neck and follow the direction of the mouth, yielding as much as the horse's stretching requires. The well-trained horse with an experienced rider will thus remain on the bit even over the jump.

When the horse's body is at the top of the jump, the landing starts, which is another critical moment. Here the rider's upper body gradually moves back, though it must not fall too soon against the horse's back. The seat bones get close to the saddle and begin to feel it, but no weight should be involved. The rider's weight becomes even more strongly supported by his knees and calves. The knees serve as a shock absorber; the rider should feel it only in his knees and not in his seat when the forelegs touch down on the ground. The elastic feeling of the ankles and feet must be maintained and no excess weight should be driven into the stirrups. If more weight is placed in the stirrups, the rider's leg will tend to swing forward, the upper body will move backward, and his weight will fall roughly against the horse's back. If, as the hind legs are touching down, the rider's seat smoothly regains its contact with the horse's back, its regularity should be restored quickly. After the second or third stride, the rider's

TAKE-OFF AND BASCULE EXERCISES

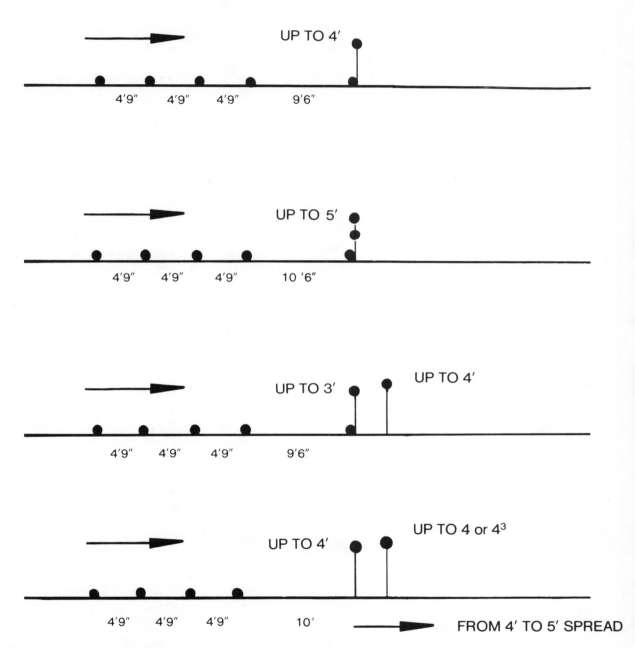

UP TO 4'

4'9" 4'9" 4'9" 9'6"

UP TO 5'

4'9" 4'9" 4'9" 10'6"

UP TO 3'   UP TO 4'

4'9" 4'9" 4'9" 9'6"

UP TO 4'   UP TO 4 or 4³

4'9" 4'9" 4'9" 10'   FROM 4' TO 5' SPREAD

Take-off and bascule exercises are beneficial for the following purposes: 1) improving the timing in approaching the first cavalletti; 2) the cavalletti makes the horse relaxed and helps it to concentrate on the ground before arriving at the take-off point; 3) the horse instinctively makes a correct bascule over the fence and properly employs its mechanism to lift its weight; 4) the rider can analyze his style over the fence. Note that in altering fences, the rear rail should be raised first; then the fence should be spread, and the front rail raised last.

110

Jumping an in-and-out: After landing, the horse makes one stride between the two elements. The horse and rider stay in perfect harmony and balance; the rider's rein contact never changes. As the horse approaches the second take-off, her position remains unchanged, her seat supporting the stride. At the second element of the combination, the horse engages its

hindquarters, lifting its body. During the take-off, the rider's seat position could be closer to the horse, but above the fence she is in a perfect position, rein contact excellent. As the horse lands, the rider's knees act as shock absorbers; her seat is close to the saddle, and a delicate rein contact is retained.

REGULATING POLE ON THE GROUND

IN FRONT AND BEHIND

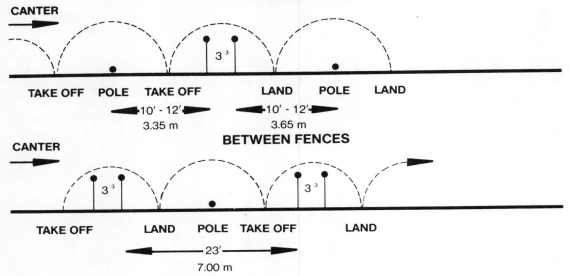

CANTER

| TAKE OFF | POLE | TAKE OFF | LAND | POLE | LAND |

10' - 12'
3.35 m

BETWEEN FENCES

CANTER

| TAKE OFF | LAND | POLE | TAKE OFF | LAND |

10' - 12'
3.65 m

23'
7.00 m

Diagram of an exercise using a regulating pole on the ground both in front of a low oxer and behind it. (This, however, can be a risky exercise with very eager horses—see text.)

position should be exactly as it was before the take-off, and the rein contact with the mouth perfectly re-established, if it was at all interrupted during the landing phase.

When the rider's position and feeling at the take-off point are secure, and the rider's style is correct, the same training can be continued at a canter. Now, instead of using the cavalletti to establish the correct take-off, we can use a low regulating fence, perhaps a pair of crossed poles, approximately one to six strides before the obstacle itself. It will be easy for the trainer and the rider to tell if the regulating fence is the right distance from the fence to be jumped, so that it does not require the even length of the horse's stride to be altered. The approach to the low regulating fence can also be controlled by a turning marker or some sort of flag, whose position can be adjusted, along with that of the regulating fence. When the turning marker is positioned properly, it permits the rider to approach the regulating fence at a canter in the proper rhythm, and the placing fence then regulates the strides evenly to the take-off point.

It is advisable to start with the regulating fence only one or two strides from the jump. The greater the number of strides between the regulating fence and the fence to jump, the more difficult it will be to maintain evenly the impulsion and length of strides so as to arrive at the proper take-off point. Gradually the regulating fence can be placed farther and farther from the fence to be jumped. And if these exercises succeed, we can eventually take away the regulating fence altogether and use only an adjusted turning marker to control the approach. Even an experienced rider will be satisfied to hit the right take-off point from six strides out.

I can recommend another exercise for controlling the take-off point, but would only use this exercise for horses that are not too quick-tempered (in other words, mostly for non-Thoroughbreds). Place a pole ten or twelve feet in front of the fence on the ground, and approach it in a steady canter. The horse will land over the pole at the right take-off point and take off immediately, making a "bounce." In performing this exercise, certain horses will speed up after landing, because they are on the forehand. This happens most frequently because the rider's upper body position has gotten ahead of the horse's center of gravity. To counteract this, and slow down this kind of horse, it may help to place a pole on the ground, ten to twelve feet behind the fence or in the middle of the distance between the in-and-out elements. However, let me reiterate that I would not use this exercise with easily excitable horses, as it will tend to make them even more eager instead of relaxed and concentrating on the task at hand.

TAKE-OFF POINT EXERCISE FROM FIVE STRIDES WITH TURNING MARKER

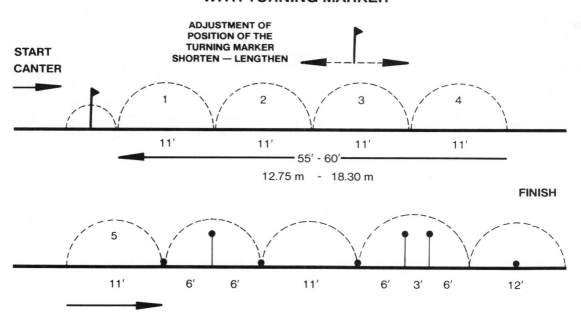

Diagram of an exercise involving five strides from a turning marker to an in-and-out. This is a difficult exercise, and it is wise to start by using only a stride or two from the marker to the fence (see text).

Neal Shapiro on Sloopy in the Munich Olympics, 1972. This picture shows the correct position. Here the rider remains close to the horse's body from his seat bones down to his heels. The rider's weight almost becomes part of the horse's own body.

Michael Matz on Jet Run in Aachen, Germany, 1978. A good landing position with weight on the knees and seat close to the saddle, but the legs have swung a bit too far back.

William (Buddy) Brown on A Little Bit at the Pan American Games, Mexico City, 1976. A good landing position, the rider maintaining light contact with open fingers. He is close to the saddle, but puts no weight on it, obviously supporting himself on his knees. The lower legs have slipped back on the sides of the horse.

10. The Gymnastic Training of the Horse

Jumper-course design has changed dramatically over the past fifty years. Today jumper courses are very much more sophisticated than they used to be, requiring better-trained horses and more skillful riders. It is hard to believe that truly satisfactory performances can be achieved over modern courses unless horses have enjoyed the preliminary groundwork of gymnastic exercises during training.

Though the term "gymnastics" is frequently heard in equestrian circles these days, I am not convinced that its principles and proper applications in training are completely understood. Gymnastics are physical exercises which aim at developing strength and agility. In addition, they should develop the power to move quickly and easily. Through gymnastic exercises, the human athlete gradually builds up muscles for his particular sport which might not otherwise be adequately developed. These exercises should not exhaust him, but rather, should help him to become more elastic, more flexible, and better coordinated.

When we apply gymnastic exercises to the horse, the objectives are identical. The horse must learn to control and adjust its own body movements. It must be able to shorten or lengthen its stride, and be able to shift its center of gravity back and forth while retaining a safe natural balance in jumping. It must develop the muscles that this kind of flexibility requires, as well as the strength to lift its own body and its rider's. Through systematic gymnastic exercises, it should also develop its own technique in jumping so that it does not have to rely on the direction of its rider. Of course, the horse must still cooperate with the rider, but through the use of the systematic gymnastic exercises, it will also learn to take care of itself.

As in cavalletti work, there are no rigid rules for the use of gymnastic exercises in training. The trainer must rely primarily upon his own common sense, imagination, observation, and flexibility. In other words, the trainer must observe the weaknesses of each individual horse and develop its program of gymnastic exercises accordingly. The training level and disposition of each particular horse must be carefully considered, especially at the beginning.

For these gymnastic exercises, several rather low- or medium-sized parallel poles will be used. These jumping elements are placed in a row at from one-stride to up to five-stride distances. The number of strides and their distances will of course vary according to the individual needs and purposes of each horse. (Elements placed more than five strides apart are no longer gymnastic exercises but serve primarily to develop the rider's timing and control in approaching the proper take-off point.)

Gymnastic training should always begin from a trot, and cavalletti are used to control the horse's impulsion and speed for its approach to the first element. The sizes of these parallel poles should not exceed four feet by four feet square, and should usually be placed even lower, especially at first. It is wise to use simple crossed poles as the first element.

The length of the natural cantering stride of each individual horse should be determined first, and its landing spot after the first obstacle should be noted. The length of one normal stride is then measured off—which takes us to the next take-off point—and the second obstacle is placed about six feet beyond. This distance will make it easy for each horse to land, make one normal stride and take off again. As we know from experience, this distance normally varies from eighteen to twenty-two feet. Horses and ponies with shorter strides will need appropriately shorter distances.

Our observation of the horses' fore- and hind legs in the air as they negotiate the second obstacle will help us judge how much we can gradually shorten the distance without changing the horse's action. In shortening the distance, adjustments of not more than four to six inches at a time are advisable. We must stop the shortening before the horse starts to twist its forelegs or drop its knees, thus being forced out of balance; if we do not, the horse may refuse or take off without making a stride.

The extent to which we can shorten the distance is limited, and the degree to which such shortening is employed thus depends very much on the size of the horse and its acrobatic abilities. If the horse should make a bad mistake, the distance must be immediately lengthened substantially, so that the horse can forget the incident and regain its confidence.

Through careful repetition, it is possible to shorten the non-jumping stride of certain horses to eight or even seven feet between two elements (making a total distance of sixteen or seventeen feet), but this extreme exercise should never be required for two consecutive strides, or if the approach is from a canter. That would be asking for trouble. I cannot emphasize enough that extremely short one-stride distances are only for certain experienced acrobatic horses; any form of "trap" must be most carefully avoided. Catching a horse through trickery is diametrically opposed to the idea of building up its confidence in its rider as well as in its own abilities. Always remember that the *normal* length of the horse's stride is between ten and twelve feet.

When the horse seems to be comfortable in jumping from a shortened stride, the dimensions of the second element can be gradually made higher and wider. If this is done with common sense, the horse will not only improve its bascule, but will also develop confidence in its own abilities and realize that it does not need to increase its speed in order to jump, but merely use the right technique along with the correct mechanics of its hindquarters. It must be remembered that it is usually easier for an untrained horse to stand back from a fence than to get too close.

When the basic "one short stride" gymnastic has been learned, an exercise with two strides may be developed, using the same principles. Begin again with a controlled approach using the cavalletti. Then, after the controlling element behind the cavalletti (the cross poles or parallel poles), the landing point and two normal strides should be calculated, and the second element placed accordingly. The procedure of gradually shortening the two-stride distance should follow, but with even more care, so that the horse will not take off after only one stride.

William Robertson on The Sheriff in Aachen, Germany, 1962. The rider's hands, the contact and upper body position are very good, but his legs have moved back slightly.

VARIATIONS OF GYMNASTIC EXERCISES

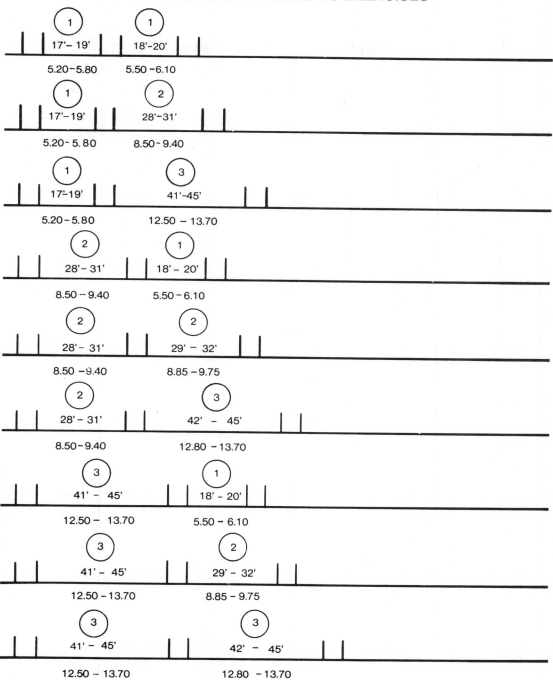

Diagram of varied gymnastics to be taken at a steady canter using one, two, and three strides in three-element combinations. The shorter and longer distances between the elements are indicated both in feet and meters.

VARIATIONS OF GYMNASTIC EXERCISES

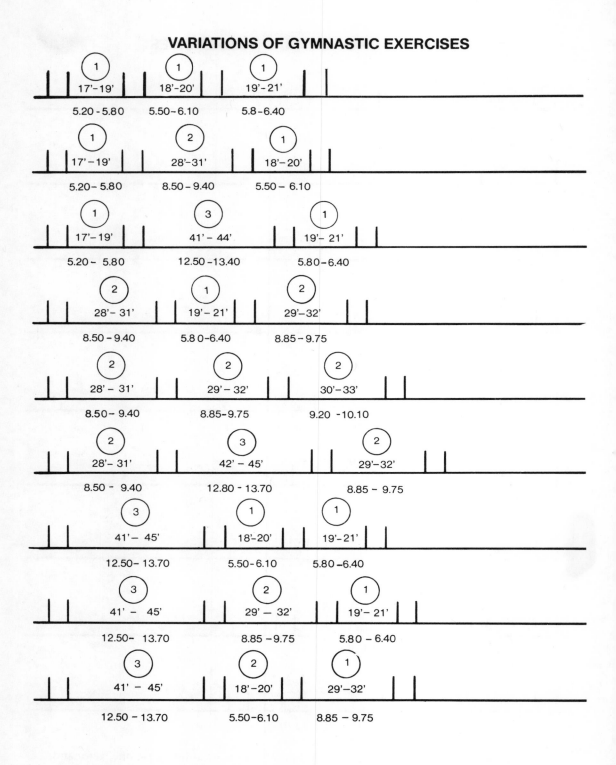

Diagram of gymnastics using variations of one, two, and three strides between four elements.

George Morris on Night Owl in Aachen, Germany, 1960. The contact with the mouth, the position of the elbows and hands are very good. The legs could be closer to the girth.

When the horse has learned how to handle short one- and two-stride distances with confidence, more short strides can be added—up to four—applying the same principles.

To balance the shortening exercises, gymnastics can also be used for lengthening the horse's strides. Usually this is easier than shortening the stride, especially for Thoroughbreds, but the horse's impulsion and take-off point should still be controlled by cavalletti. The horse must be trained to lengthen its strides, not by increasing its speed, but by using better mechanics. Landing after the first element with its rider's encouragement, it must be trained to stretch out and extend its stride.

I do not recommend demanding lengthening for more than one or two strides if the first obstacle is approached from a trot. Asking for additional lengthened strides can cause the horse to lose its improved bascule, and teach it to become flat over the jump.

To summarize, these gymnastic exercises should be repeated until they are routine. Some horses will learn and develop faster than others. Hastening the training will never pay off. We should always begin by first setting the distance for one normal stride before requiring more.

Once the horse has mastered the trotting approach through the cavalletti to the crossed poles, it will be ready to do without the cavalletti and

GYMNASTIC EXERCISES

ONE STRIDE

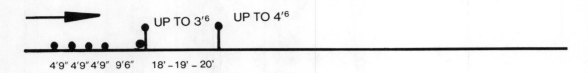

UP TO 3'6   UP TO 4'6

4'9" 4'9" 4'9" 9'6"   18'–19'–20'

ONE STRIDE

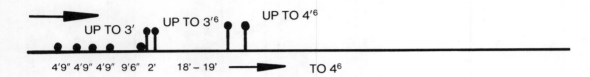

UP TO 3'   UP TO 3'6   UP TO 4'6

4'9" 4'9" 4'9" 9'6" 2'   18'–19'   TO 4⁶

TWO STRIDE

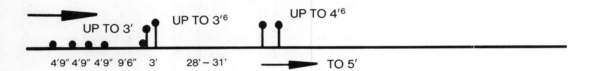

UP TO 3'   UP TO 3'6   UP TO 4'6

4'9" 4'9" 4'9" 9'6" 3'   28'–31'   TO 5'

THREE STRIDE

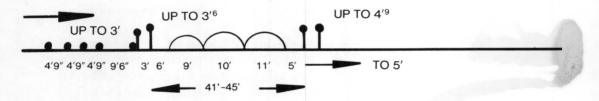

UP TO 3'   UP TO 3'6   UP TO 4'9

4'9" 4'9" 4'9" 9'6" 3' 6'   9'   10'   11'   5'   TO 5'

41'-45'

FOUR STRIDE

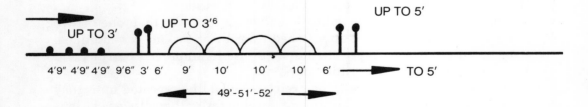

UP TO 3'   UP TO 3'6   UP TO 5'

4'9" 4'9" 4'9" 9'6" 3' 6'   9'   10'   10'   10'   6'   TO 5'

49'-51'-52'

Diagrammatic portrayal of the basic exercises for regulating one, two, three, and four strides between two elements. The approaches are controlled by the cavalletti.

approach the crossed poles directly in a steady, somewhat collected canter, starting from not too far away—perhaps only six or seven strides. The rider should concentrate on arriving at the right take-off point. It is still best to use crossed poles as the regulating fence, followed by basic normal strides between elements, i.e., eighteen to twenty feet for one stride, thirty to thirty-two feet for two. We must remember that we used short distances to improve the horse's bascule, and controlled the horse's impulsion during the approach to facilitate it. In contrast, very short strides should not be used from a canter; the horse will not be able to maintain the same rhythm and will either move faster and faster or simply leave out one stride. In all training, but especially when altering distances in the gymnastics, we must remain open-minded. Adjustments are a necessity, but a lengthened stride at the canter should not be demanded for more than one or two strides, and must be immediately followed with one or two shorter strides.

Variation in the number of strides between the elements is the next phase of the gymnastic exercises. The exercises with differing numbers of strides and distances will challenge the trainer's imagination, for he must think about what kind of gymnastic is needed for each individual horse. The previous discussion should give the trainer enough bases on which to create his own variations. Careful study of the examples of gymnastic courses (see Appendix, Nos. 1-22) is also recommended. It should always be remembered that the horse's confidence must be preserved at all costs. Mistakes should be rectified with patience and corrected with repetitions of easier gymnastics.

While the principles for gymnastic exercises have now been described in detail, one possible area of confusion should be clarified. It will be noted that our gymnastic diagrams show a maximum of only four elements. In practice, the number of elements employed need not be limited; there can be five or even more elements, as well as differing numbers and various lengths of strides. In many situations, of course, using more than four obstacles is not very practical, but we will leave this up to the judgment of the trainer or rider.

Finally, I would like to stress again that it is important, when using shorter and longer strides, to still never trap the horse. However, when the horse shows complete confidence in handling the gymnastics, it is a good idea occasionally to make a sudden test by raising the last element substantially. Since the horse will be unprepared for this sudden change in the dimensions of the last fence, its rider should be even more ready with strong support from his seat, and very careful not to lose contact with or drop the reins. The practical benefit of this test is that both rider and horse will learn that a big fence can be jumped from a short stride and close take-off distance, provided that the horse is trained to use the correct technique and the rider is in harmony with it.

GYMNASTIC VARIATIONS

SHORT ONE LONG	SHORT ONE LONG	SHORT TWO LONG
17' - 19' 5.20 - 5.80	18' - 20' 5.50 - 6.10	29' - 32' 8.80 - 9.70
ONE 17' - 19' 5.20 - 5.80	TWO 28' - 31' 8.50 - 9.40	THREE 41' - 45' 12.50 - 13.70
ONE 17' - 19' 5.20 - 5.80	THREE 41' - 45' 12.50 - 13.70	THREE 42' - 45' 12.80 - 13.80
TWO 28' - 31' 8.50 - 9.40	ONE 18' - 20' 5.50 - 6.10	ONE 19' - 21' 5.80 - 6.40
TWO 28' - 31' 8.50 - 9.40	TWO 29' - 32' 8.80 - 9.70	ONE 19' - 21' 5.80 - 6.40
TWO 28' - 31' 8.50 - 9.40	THREE 41' - 45' 12.50 - 13.70	ONE 19' - 21' 5.80 - 6.40
THREE 41' - 45' 12.50 - 13.70	ONE 18' - 20' 5.50 - 6.10	ONE 19' - 21' 5.50 - 6.40
THREE 41' - 45' 12.50 - 13.70	TWO 28' - 31' 8.50 - 9.40	ONE 19' - 21' 5.50 - 6.40
THREE 41' - 45' 12.50 - 13.70	THREE 42' - 45' 12.80 - 13.70	ONE 19' - 21' 5.50 - 6.40

Diagram of various numbers of strides, up to a total of seven. Distances between elements are given for both short and long strides.

GYMNASTIC VARIATIONS

NUMBER OF STRIDES		
SHORT ONE LONG 17' - 19' 5.20 – 5.80	SHORT ONE LONG 18' - 20' 5.50 – 6.10	SHORT THREE LONG 41' 45' 12 .50 – 13.70
ONE 17' - 19' 5.20 – 5.80	THREE 41'– 45' 12 .50 – 13.70	ONE 19' - 21' 5.80 – 6.40
ONE 17' - 19' 5.20 – 5.80	THREE 41' – 45' 12.50 –13.70	TWO 29' - 32' 8.85 – 9.75
ONE 17' - 19' 5.20 – 5.80	FOUR 49' - 52' 15.00 –15.85	ONE 19' - 21' 5.80 – 6.40
FOUR 49' - 52' 15.00 – 15.85	ONE 18' - 20' 5.50 – 6.10	ONE 19' - 21' 5.80 – 6.40
FOUR 49' - 52' 15.00 – 15.85	TWO 28' - 31' 8.50 – 9.40	ONE 19' - 21' 5.80 - 6.40
FOUR 49' - 52' 15.00 – 15.85	ONE 18' - 20' 5.50 – 6.10	TWO 29' - 32' 8.85 – 9.75
FOUR 49' - 52' 15.00 – 15.85	ONE 18' - 20' 5.50 – 6.10	THREE 42' - 45' 12.80-13.70

Diagram of various numbers of strides, up to a total of eight.

Riding a gymnastic exercise: While approaching the take-off point, the rider's upper body remains still, waiting for the horse's hind legs to move over the last cavalletti.

Over the first fence, the rider's position is perfect; straight back, seat close to the saddle, knee and leg position is unchanged, hands deep, and a straight line from the bit to the rider's elbow.

Landing: The rider's position is correct. She feels the saddle, but her weight is on her knees and calves. The rein contact is unchanged.

Upon landing, the rider picks up the stride with her seat, and supports the stride between fences with her seat. The rein contact remains perfect.

Supporting the stride between elements, with seat and rein contact unchanged.

During the take-off at the second fence, the upper body bends a bit more forward, because the fence is higher and wider.

The rider's position over the fence is in full harmony with the horse's center of gravity.

In landing, her upper body starts to move back, but her weight remains on her knees while her legs remain in their original position against the sides of the horse.

Some horses with good jumping ability are either careless by nature or develop a certain laziness over a period of time, and do not make enough effort to clear the jumps. Prior to competition a skilled trainer can alleviate this character flaw, at least temporarily, by carefully following by eye the position of the front and hind legs in the air over an oxer. Working with an experienced rider who possesses the ability to approach the fence with exactly the same rhythm each time, the trainer gradually moves the rear poles of the oxers backwards, a few inches at a time, until the horse touches or knocks down the pole. This will make a sensitive horse just careful enough to jump more cleanly in the competition to follow.

Rapping the horse from the ground with a bamboo pole, or purposely crashing it into a fence, does not improve the horse's confidence or concentration, and very often creates more problems than it solves. In fact, I regard such actions as detrimental preparation that stand against all accepted basic principles of training, even though they are still widely employed by some riders and trainers.

11. Schooling and Competing over Courses

Warming Up

The ultimate goal of most jumper training is a successful competitive performance. Even with the most careful training, however, the competition itself will be wasted unless the horse is given an intelligent preparation during the warm-up, for many classes are lost right there. The ideal warm-up time will vary from horse to horse, but it should never extend so long that the horse becomes too tired to perform at its best. The horse's freshness and interest must always be preserved. In addition, its disposition must be taken into consideration, as well as the type of competition which is to follow.

In warming up we should first attempt to make the horse responsive to the fundamental aids, while still keeping it mentally relaxed. Next, we should jump a couple of low fences, combined with some transitions and sharp turns. This exercise will serve as adequate preparation for jumping a couple of higher upright fences and, from a very steady canter, a wider oxer.

The preparation of horses with difficult dispositions, on the other hand, must be approached differently. Some horses become very excited when other riders are cantering and jumping fences in all directions in the warm-up area. The noise of knocked-down rails is especially disturbing for such horses, and their preparation must be handled in a different and more carefully planned manner, avoiding all disadvantageous circumstances as much as possible. Ideally we should find a quieter place to warm up, but such a location usually is not readily available. If that is the case, it may help to put this kind of horse on the longe line, using proper side lines or draw reins, and to longe it over poles on the ground. This kind of activity encourages horses to relax, since their attention is directed away from all other preoccupations, and they then need only to jump a few fences before entering the ring. Horses with even more difficult dispositions may have to be ridden or longed well in advance of the competition, and then perhaps hand-walked until the moment they enter the ring.

Whatever the horse's temperament, its warm-up preparation prior to competition should be adjusted imaginatively. Any confrontation should be avoided; intelligent compromise will better serve both horse and rider. Remember that the warm-up area is not the place to hope to change the disposition or level of training of a horse.

The type of competition for which one is getting ready will also make a difference in one's preparation. For a speed competition involving twisting and sharp turns, transitions with a sudden increase of speed, and lengthening of strides in a canter for short distances can serve as useful schooling exercises.

In contrast, for a puissance competition (the jumping of big single fences), collected canter work and concentration on the timing and take-off points from a straight line will be more appropriate.

The Diagram of the Course

In addition to warming up his horse, there are other important matters for the rider to attend to before the competition. One of them is studying the course diagram which is posted before the course is opened for inspection.

The rider should take time to become acquainted with the course of the competition from the diagram. He should check the position of the starting and finishing lines, and consider the advantages of approaching them from different angles. He should note the required rate of speed and the time allowed, and if there is a chance to observe a few of the first competitors, he should verify how tightly the time "rides" so that he can avoid possible time faults. (In addition, he should study from the chart the jump-off line, if any, so that he can walk that, too, after walking the original course.) Remember that the course diagram is not always accurate in every respect, and must be rechecked against the actual course.

All these details take time, but we should never underestimate their importance. Once the course is open for inspection, the rider can use his time much more economically if he already knows what to expect.

Inspecting the Course

By now, the rider must know the length of his own stride, as well as the usual cantering stride of his horse. Having located the starting line and determined the best direction from which to approach the first fence, the rider now follows the line of the course from fence to fence. The contour of the ground and possible soft spots must be noted, for uneven ground will often alter ordinary calculations of strides.

In walking, the rider will notice that some of the fences are related to each other in striding, requiring a stride to be added or left out. This can only be discovered by walking the course and not from looking at the diagram. In general, fences spaced within six or seven strides from each other are usually related and require special attention.

Depending on the type and size of fences, as well as the horse's stride and manner of jumping, the rider should be able to locate the horse's expected take-off point and the probable landing point. From the landing point, the rider, by counting his own steps, can determine the number of normal horse-strides it will take to get to the next take-off point, and thus translate the distance between the fences into the correct number of strides.

Additional factors which must be taken into consideration include such things as the composition of the footing and any variation of the ground. Is it hard or soft, heavy or slippery? All these circumstances will influence the rider's final judgments and decisions. Should he maintain an even rhythm between the fences, or take a more collected approach, and add an extra stride in between? Or perhaps, if it is a jump-off, the rider will choose the other option, and lengthen the stride so that he can leave a stride out.

When fences are separated from each other by more than seven strides, determining how to approach them will not be difficult even for less expe-

Frank Chapot on Trail Guide in Rome, Olympic Games, 1960.

rienced riders. In general, however, the fewer the strides between fences, the more difficult the rider's decision. Take every chance to observe other competitors ride the course, especially the good ones, for quite often their experiences will influence your original judgment.

The combinations—the double and triple fences with one or two strides between them in various distances—are usually the highlights of the course, and require the most attention from the competitors. It is easier to decide how to ride them if they are not also related to other fences coming before or after them. Again, one's decision regarding how to ride these combinations will be based on the expected take-off and landing points, as influenced by the horse's normal length of stride in a canter. The length of stride required between elements will be controlled by the amount of impulsion with which the combination is approached.

When the combinations are also related to the fences before or after them, the approach must be more sophisticated, demanding more from the rider's skill and experience. The use of gymnastic exercises during the horse's previous training will truly pay off here, for it will be reflected in how well the horse responds to its rider's requests to shorten or lengthen its stride. One basic principle must be remembered in this regard: After the landing, especially in combinations, the first stride's length must always be controlled, whether that stride is to be long or short. It is safer and easier to make adjustments at that point than it is to waste the landing stride, leaving any adjustments to the very last stride before jumping.

After the entire course has been inspected, it is a good idea to return to any problem spots or difficult turns, and to recheck one's first impressions and planned execution. Since there will be no special time for inspecting the jump-off course, one should first concentrate upon the original course and then analyze the jump-off course separately. In the jump-off course it is obviously most important to figure out the shortest lines and turns, and any possible options that the rider might be able to employ, such as turning inside a certain fence instead of going around it. Of course, it is also important to determine the shortest distance from the last fence to the finish line, for this often makes the difference between the winner and the loser in actual competition.

Entering the Show Ring

The most important point to remember about entering the show ring is to go through the in-gate with lively impulsion, keeping the horse attentive but relaxed. Some horses are naturally easy and confident, and present no problems when faced with new situations. Other horses, however, become tense and suspicious, and are easily frightened by noises and lots of people.

With horses of normal disposition, quick transitions, short extensions, and a few rein-back steps before saluting the judges works out well. Before striking off in a canter, several leg-yieldings will also ensure the horse's acceptance of the rider's leg signals. Then the first fence should be approached in a slightly collected, well-balanced frame.

With suspicious, withholding horses, on the other hand, their hesitation must be overcome by entering at a strong, forceful canter. Highly excitable horses require special patience and quiet handling, and should be given a longer chance to look around, thus avoiding anything that might be upsetting. They will need some time to become familiar and confident in the new surroundings before they begin the competition. (Remember, however, that the rules permit only one minute between the salute and crossing the starting line.)

Riding the Course

The fences in jumping courses are usually evenly distributed with several changes of direction in the line. About half—preferably not more—of the fences will be related to each other with different distances, including the combinations. Thanks to a well-planned warm-up and a careful study of the course diagram, followed by the inspection of the course on foot, the rider should be free to concentrate only on his riding while actually jumping the course. His concentration should focus continuously upon preserving the horse's natural balance and correct rhythm, in accordance with the required speed as well as the sizes of the fences.

Maintaining the horse's natural balance while proceeding on a straight line requires the rider's weight to be distributed evenly and correctly. However, adjustments will often be necessary before the correct take-off point is approached, as well as after the landing. Such readjustments of the rider's position must be smooth and gradual, and the rider's weight must never be shifted suddenly ahead of the base of the support area. If this should happen, the horse will lose its balance, get on the forehand and, to regain its balance, accelerate its movement, while any exaggerated movement backward will result only in a defensive reaction from the horse.

Proper rhythm and impulsion are essential to accurate timing of the take-off. Only the most experienced jumping riders can keep their horses in perfect balance and in a suitable rhythm over a jumping course of seventeen to twenty obstacles. Even so, 15 to 20 percent of their take-off points may prove slightly too close to the fence, or slightly too far. In such situations, the rider and horse will still succeed in jumping the fences cleanly if they both have been previously trained through gymnastic exercises, and have learned the right techniques.

If any adjustment is necessary in rhythm and impulsion, there are only two alternatives—shortening or lengthening the strides. Experience shows that it usually is preferable to gradually lengthen the stride in approaching a fence instead of taking back, but again, such determinations will depend upon each individual rider's timing and his horse's particular abilities. The more experienced the rider the farther away from the obstacle he will be able to make his decision.

Turns

Along with the horse's warm-up, the subject of properly executed turns is seldom emphasized strongly enough, and is often regarded as much simpler than it really is. Yet in fact, poorly executed turns, in which the horse loses its natural balance, are among the most common causes of faults at the subsequent fence, and often prove critical in competitions against the clock as well.

First of all, it must be recognized that turning the horse in a new direction always requires more than simply pulling the rein on that side. It is of the utmost importance that we learn the technique of executing turns properly, since every jumper course will require this maneuver, and some of the turns the courses demand may be very difficult.

As mentioned earlier, certain elementary training movements provide particularly good preparation for teaching the horse to turn correctly and safely. These exercises consist of the shoulder-in, haunches-in, turn-on-the-haunches, and the two-track movements. Always remember that the turn does not consist solely of a single curved line, for while the horse's inside legs are moving on one line, its outside legs are moving along a distinct and separate parallel line. As its body shortens along the inside line, it must stretch along the outside line. Also, in order to make a good turn, the rider must concentrate on not losing the horse's natural balance while still maintaining its regularity of motion in the new direction.

There are specific exercises which can be employed in training the horse to initiate proper turns, and to continue along the curve of the turn with the control and support of the rider. Such turning exercises should first be introduced at a walk, and later at a trot. Similarly, such training should begin first on a large circle, which should gradually be reduced in diameter as training progresses.

To begin, the weight of the rider's body is shifted toward the side of the direction of the turn, always in coordinated harmony with the degree of the turn. The rider then must draw the horse's head and neck in the

(Opposite) Exercise of a sharp turn to the left: The horse's hind legs are moving along a very small circle, its inside hind leg very well engaged, the horse appearing to be in stable balance. The rider's position is correct, his weight well on the inside seat bone, and the horse's outside shoulder and hind legs are well under his control.

direction of the turn by using repeated soft pulls on the inside rein, while still passively resisting with the outside rein in order to control the outside shoulder, and counteracting with the inside rein to prevent the inside shoulder from falling inward. It is clear that in any turn both reins are involved in serving a leveling function for the horse—to keep the horse on the curve, and also maintain its natural balance.

The rider's inside leg should preserve the horse's impulsion while his outside leg prevents any deviation of the horse's outside hind leg. The sharper the turn, the more strongly the support of the outside leg must be applied.

The most common failure of riders in competition is starting the turns too late. The following concept is very helpful in solving this problem. First, imagine a center line in the middle of each obstacle on the course. In principle, each fence should be jumped at this center line if the approach is straight. However, if the approach is from a turn, the line of that turn should not pass the imaginary center line. Why is this so? The explanation is that the horse's leading (inside) shoulder must be free to jump at the take-off point, and should not be pulled back by the rider, as might be necessary to hold the horse on the center line of the fence. Such pulling would also interfere with the horse's balance, and perhaps even result in a change of lead or a crossing of its hind legs before the take-off.

Speed is another important factor to consider during turns. In order to keep the horse well balanced in the turns, especially in sharp turns, its rider must decrease speed before turning toward the new direction. Such deceleration must not, however, interfere with the maintenance of the horse's lively rhythm. A practical analogy might be that of driving a car through a turn by gearing down. As in road racing, the correct technique of executing a turn is to brake (shorten and collect) on the approach to the turn, and then, as the turn is completed, to accelerate (lengthening the stride).

While many riders are uncomfortable when jumping from a turn, there is a distinct advantage in it. Most riders seem to feel that it is easier to approach a fence from a straight line because they feel more secure in their timing of the take-off point. This may be valid for most riders, but it is certainly not so for the cleverer ones. For the latter, the approach to the fence from a turn offers very helpful options, for the turn lets them choose the best take-off point from anywhere along the face of the fence, reducing or increasing the distance, depending upon each individual horse's speed, rhythm, and jumping technique. Such options give the flexible, experienced rider and a well-trained horse a clear edge over a less-experienced rider who has less confidence in his eye and his horse.

Special Types of Obstacles

In addition to the ordinary vertical and spread fences which we have already dealt with in detail, there is also a category of "special" obstacles which remains to be discussed. These special types of obstacles—primarily water jumps, banks, dry ditches, and liverpools—have an entirely different character from other fences, and require certain adjustments in the rider's timing and riding. Since they are not (and should not be) used very often in ordinary competitions, neither horses nor riders become as familiar with them as they do with the usual verticals and spreads, and thus they require special attention in schooling.

Although these special fences on occasion cause a lot of faults, they are not more difficult than ordinary fences—on the contrary, they are generally easier, even though different. It is usually their novelty that causes problems, rather than any intrinsic difficulty. Do not expect your horse to master them in a single session, or to deal with them immediately in their most difficult forms. The key to developing a good water-, bank-, or ditch-jumping technique is working progressively, starting with the obstacles in their simplest, easiest forms, just as we have done with regular fences. (Nobody expects a horse to progress from jumping cross-rails to five-foot verticals in a single afternoon, but I have seen riders choose a twelve- to fifteen-foot water as their first effort over this type of obstacle, "to see if it can jump water"!)

The Water Jump

Of all the special obstacles, only the water jump requires any special talent on the part of the horse, or at least a special attitude, and very often it is the horse that basically doesn't like water—and thus respects it—that makes the best water jumper. Whatever the reason, it is clear that certain individual horses have an exceptional instinct to jump the water easily and carefully. They want to land well on the other side of the water, not in it. However, if they jump the water too often (and especially, if they are asked to jump badly constructed water jumps) they lose interest in making the effort required to land cleanly on the other side of the water. Sometimes they can see the bottom, and, realizing that the water is not deep, become careless. The more often the horse makes a mistake the more its rider tends to develop a complex, and loses his confidence in how to approach the water. Such riders frequently start too early to increase their speed and impulsion in approaching the take-off point. Obviously, the horse will need increased speed to clear a wide water jump, but if the

Mary Mairs Chapot on White Lightning in Hickstead, England, 1967.

Chrystine Jones on Toy Soldier in Hickstead, England, 1967.

William (Buddy) Brown on Viscount in Aachen, Germany, 1976.

Robert Ridland on Almost Persuaded in Aachen, Germany, 1971.

increase in impulsion starts too early, it will tend to gradually decrease instead, and there will be insufficient thrust at the moment when it is necessary to lengthen the stride over the water.

The opposite approach can also produce a fault. If the rider underestimates the width of the water or overestimates the scope of his horse and starts too late to increase speed, he will lack sufficient momentum for the ultimate adjustment. The experienced rider will first speed up for the approach and then collect for the timing; when he can see the distance for the take-off, he will energetically increase impulsion with strong seat support, not losing rein contact, but rather, stabilizing it. It is a mistake to try to interfere with the last stride or two with a sudden decrease in impulsion. If the timing is not perfect, lengthening the stride generally affords a better chance at a successful jump. It is a good idea to try to place the take-off as close to the edge of the water as is possible, without breaking the momentum of the stride; in any case, "standing back" at the water jump— taking off from too far away—must be avoided. In general, horses that have an instinct to make a powerful, short stride just before the take-off, without losing their impulsion, are the best water jumpers. Nearly every horse becomes a bit unbalanced after landing over the water, and needs a couple of strides to shift its center of gravity backward. The rider's position must coordinate with this shift immediately in order to assist the horse in reestablishing its natural balance.

Horses should not be schooled over the water very often, and when they are, a light wooden rail about two inches in diameter should be placed halfway across, about two feet above the water's surface. Rather, the horse should meet an open water only in competition.

Banks

Another "special" ingredient of certain jumper courses is the bank. In the past, permanent banks gave a particular character to many different horse-show grounds. They were designed and constructed very differently from each other, and individual preparation for them by horses and riders was not always possible.

Unfortunately, almost all of these varied banks and bank combinations have been eliminated in the last twenty years, and those that remain are mostly copies of each other. One reason why so few are left is that it was not possible for riders to practice over them before competition, thus giving local participants a competitive advantage over the "outsiders." Consequently, the banks that remain are usually restricted to special competitions such as derby courses and certain speed classes. My experience is that for horses in general, jumping up and down banks seems to be quite natural. Even so, banks should be introduced gradually, beginning with small ones. As soon as a horse becomes thoroughly familiar with the basic kinds of banks, it should be able to handle their many variations without difficulty, even those connected with combinations.

The best way to think about jumping a bank is to visualize a medium-sized, fairly wide oxer. One must make sure to increase impulsion, and stand back somewhat at the take-off point; the horse should then land with its forelegs well on top of the bank, so that its hind legs have plenty of ground on which to land and do not strike short of the edge of the bank. When the horse loses impulsion and gets too close to the bottom of the bank, its forelegs will get onto the bank, but its hind legs will fail to do so because of insufficient impulsion and space, and the horse will land with its belly on the edge of the bank. This is a serious situation in which the horse can be badly hurt. It should be kept in mind that fluent, but not extremely forward riding, together with a deep landing on the top of the bank, is the correct tactic.

Once the horse is safely on the bank, it should not be given any chance to slow down or hesitate. The rider must make sure the horse keeps going, continuing its movement to get off of the bank. Out of surprise, horses sometimes hesitate to jump off, which can result in a penalty for a refusal, especially if there is a ditch on the landing side, which is not uncommon.

Kathy Kusner on Untouchable in Hickstead, England, 1968. An exceptional example of the correct way to jump up on a bank.

The rider must pay very close attention to his contact with the horse's mouth. As the horse jumps up and down over a bank, perhaps even "bouncing" it without a stride, it will be very difficult for even the best rider to avoid interfering with the horse's mouth. This is a situation in which a rider may prefer to lose rein contact completely, and even grab a piece of mane.

Ditches

Dry ditches are probably the least common of the special obstacles, and, like banks, are most likely to be encountered as an element in derby or speed courses. They do not really require any special riding approach, though it is important that they should have been introduced gradually. A ditch only three feet wide is quite enough for the horse's first encounter, and it should be encouraged to walk up and inspect it, and even put its

(Left) Frank D. Chapot on Anakonda in Hickstead, England, 1967. The rider's position is classic, his center of gravity is perfectly above the horse's center of gravity. His legs are right on the side of the horse and the contact with the reins is exemplary. (Right) Neal Shapiro on Uncle Max in Hickstead, England, 1968. The rider's position is unorthodox, however an excited or inexperienced horse can unexpectedly leave the bank. Even so, this rider is not disturbing the horse.

head down in it and smell it. Such small ditches should then be tried from a trot, with gentle encouragement or even a light touch with the whip, and after brief hesitation every horse should be able to get to the other side, since such a narrow obstacle can be negotiated from even a walk or stand-still if necessary.

Deeper and wider ditches can be more impressive and even frightening for certain young horses, and this is especially true if the ditch has not been turfed, but is deep and dark at the bottom; most young horses will then regard it with suspicion. The best advice is to take lots of time and use lots of patience, and to increase the difficulty of the ditches only gradually. A rail placed a foot to eighteen inches above the surface in the middle of the ditch is often a useful aid. Once the horse has no hesitation in jumping the ditch at a trot, it can be negotiated at a canter.

The key to riding big ditches, as with the water jump, is to try *not* to stand back, but to find a take-off point close to the edge of the ditch. The horse's forward motion should not be broken, and a fluent rhythm as well as frank contact with the horse's mouth should be maintained.

Vertical rails placed in the middle of a dry ditch will cause few horses any difficulty. However, a wide, parallel oxer built over it which enables the horse to still see the deepness of the ditch will require very firm, determined support during the approach. Indeed, something of an optical illusion seems to be involved, for an oxer with a ditch underneath rides as a larger fence than it would by itself, and both horse and rider must be prepared mentally as well as physically to cope with it.

Liverpools

The liverpool is basically a shallow water about six feet in width which is most often used in conjunction with other fence elements, and often in combinations. It should rarely cause any problems unless the horse is par-ticularly suspicious of water. Permanent pairs of liverpools still exist on a few show-jumping grounds (Aachen and Hickstead, for example), but temporary, moveable ones constructed of rubber are much more com-monly encountered these days. They have the advantage of providing the course designer with much more flexibility, and their varying placement can contribute much to the challenge and interest of the course. Though liverpools are not intrinsically difficult, since they "fit" comfortably under the arc of a normal jump, a pair of oxers built over a pair of liverpools will require accurate riding in the approach, and demand both confidence and obedience from the horse.

When vertical fences (rails or planks, but never a gate) are placed on the near side of liverpools, there is no need to ride them differently than one would ride the vertical by itself. Similarly, triple bars are basically easy, and only the "true" liverpool, with a vertical on the far side of the water, can sometimes cause a problem if the horse holds back and cannot be placed in a good take-off spot, close to the edge of the water. In general, it is important that horses become sufficiently familiar with water, as with ditches, to be able to virtually ignore them, and concentrate on the rails instead. Incidentally, it is worth occasional schooling over a liverpool that follows a solid fence—such as a wall—in combination, for the horse that basically dislikes water may prove most vulnerable to liverpools that cannot be seen in advance and so come as a surprise at the last minute.

Perhaps in this modern era it is sometimes necessary to take certain short cuts, but classic principles should never be compromised. No method is perfect in any activity in life, but a systematic method is always better than simply following a personal preference.

The objective of victory in any competition is important. It animates the spirit, confidence and ambition of the individual. However, the good feeling of having performed well is better than any temporary success.

Left to right: Bertalan de Némethy, standing; William C. Steinkraus, Individual Olympic Gold Medal in 1968, on Fleet Apple; Neal Shapiro, Individual Olympic Bronze Medal in 1972, on Sloopy; Joe Fargis IV, Individual Olympic Gold Medal in 1984, on Bonte II; Conrad Homfeld, Individual Olympic Silver Medal in 1984, on Triple Crown (Aachen, Germany, 1971).

Appendix

Gymnastic Courses

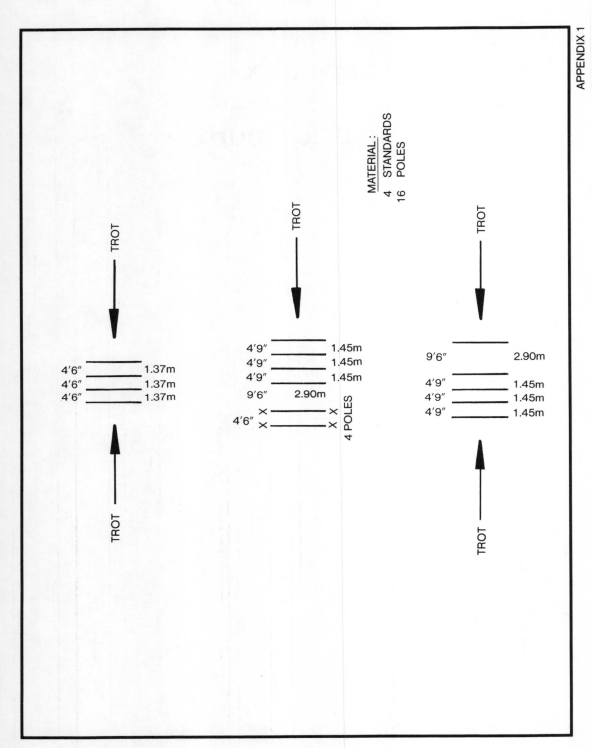

APPENDIX 1

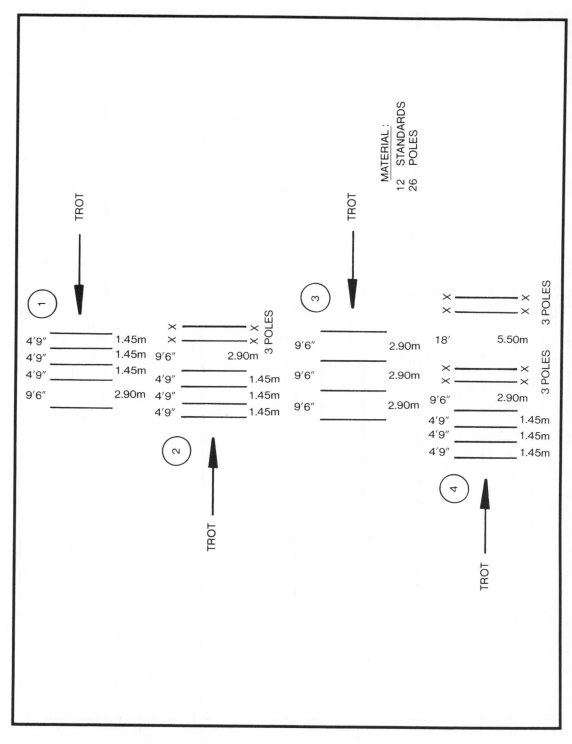

APPENDIX 2

Appendix

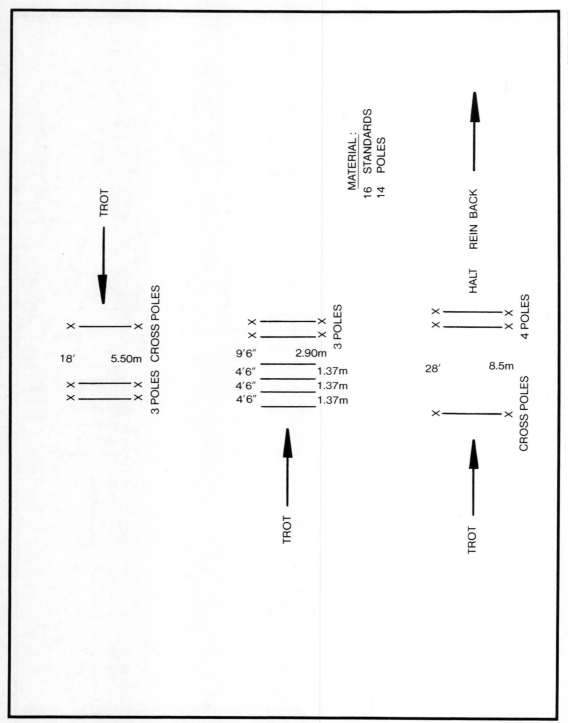

APPENDIX 3

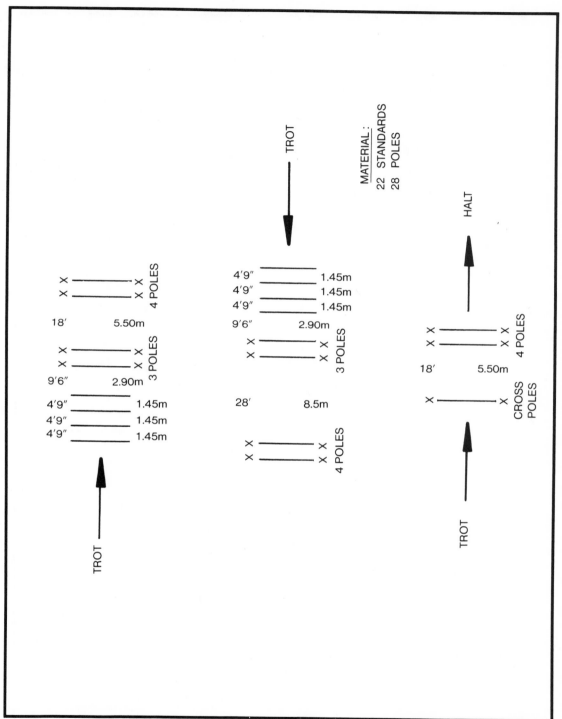

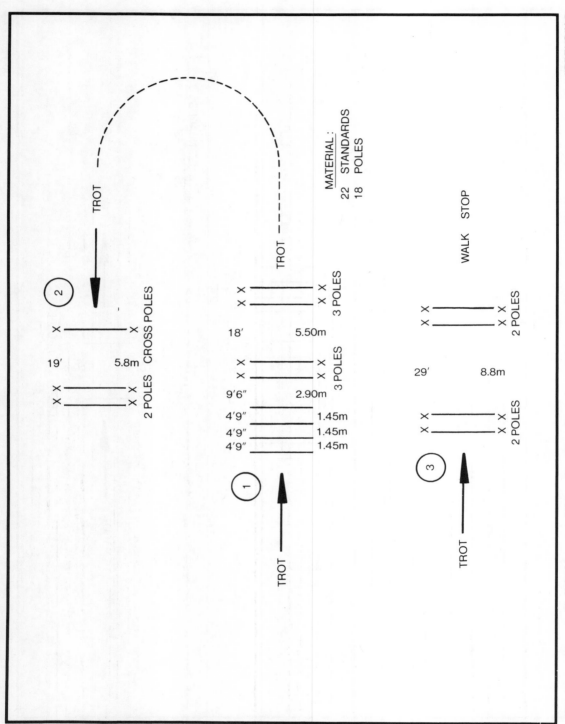

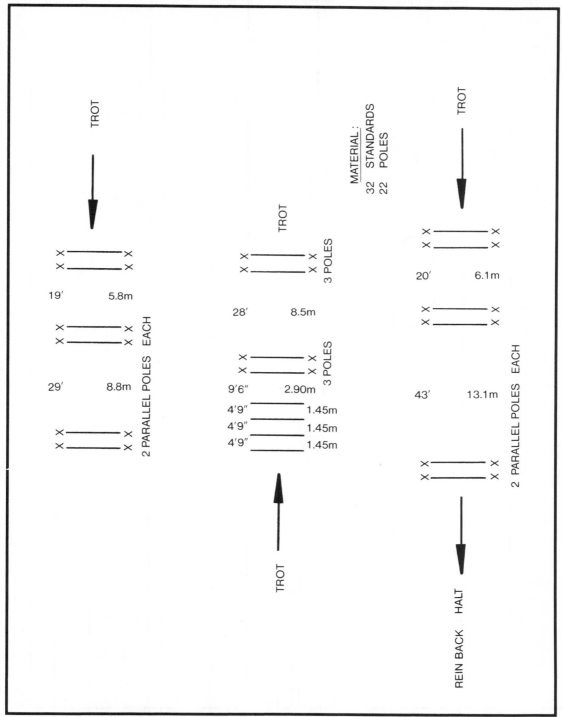

APPENDIX 6

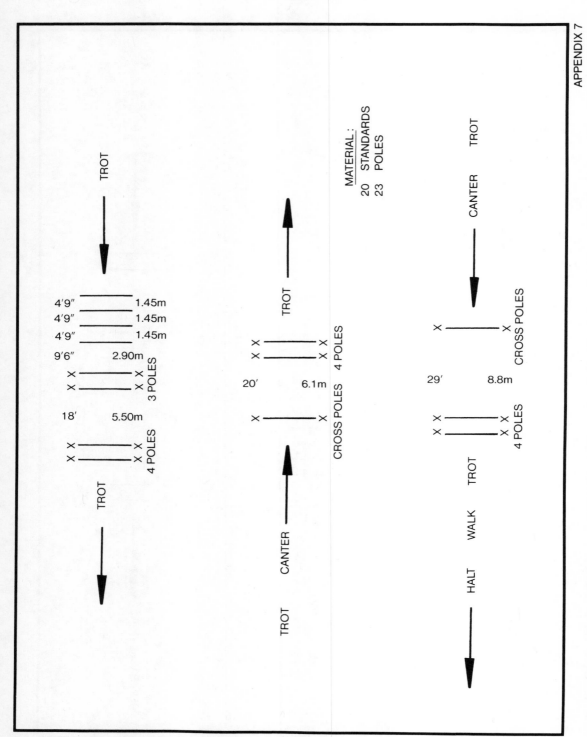

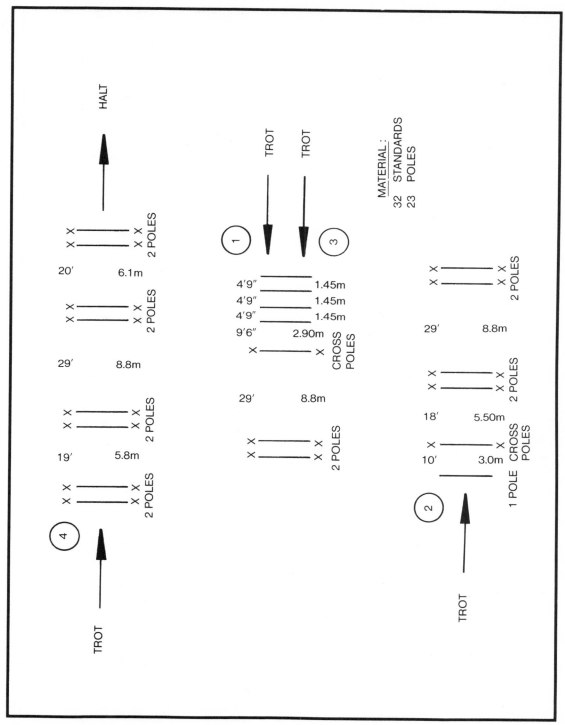

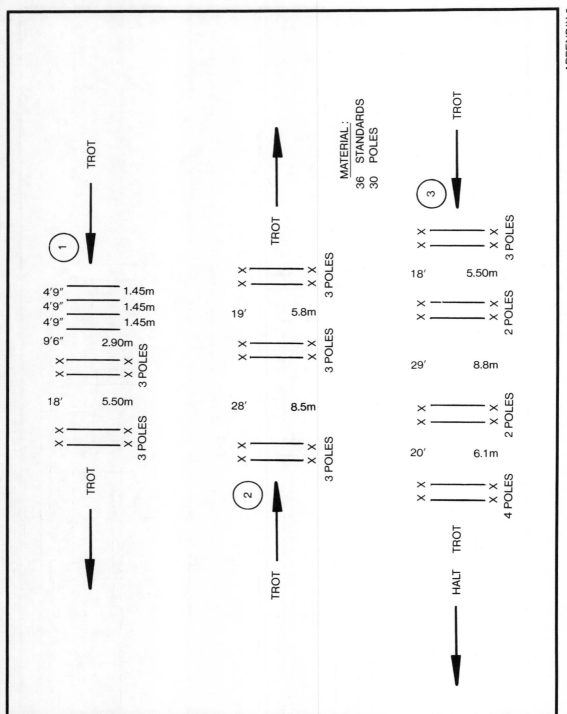

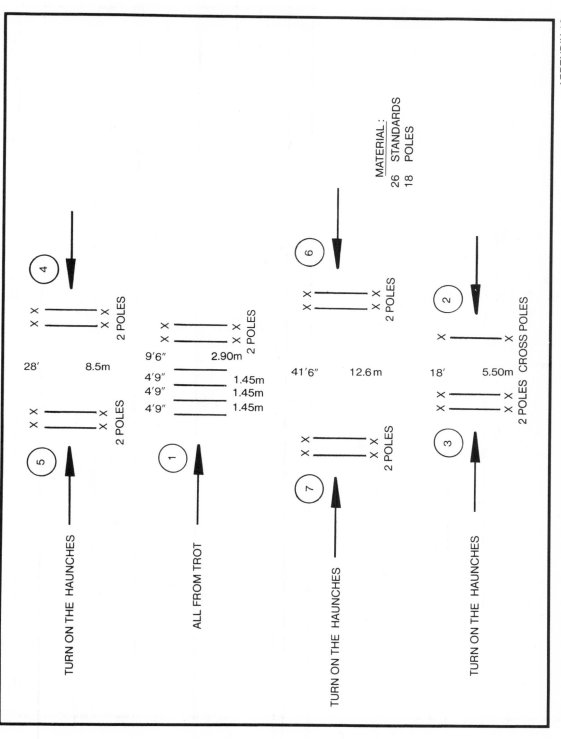

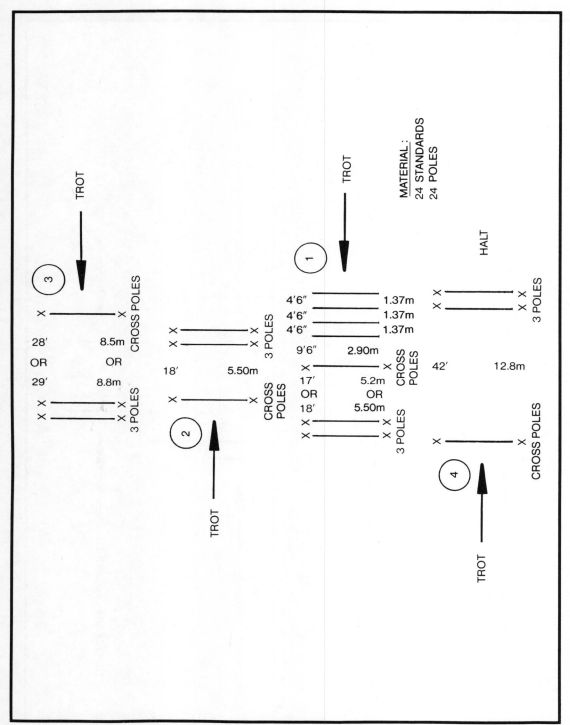

APPENDIX 11

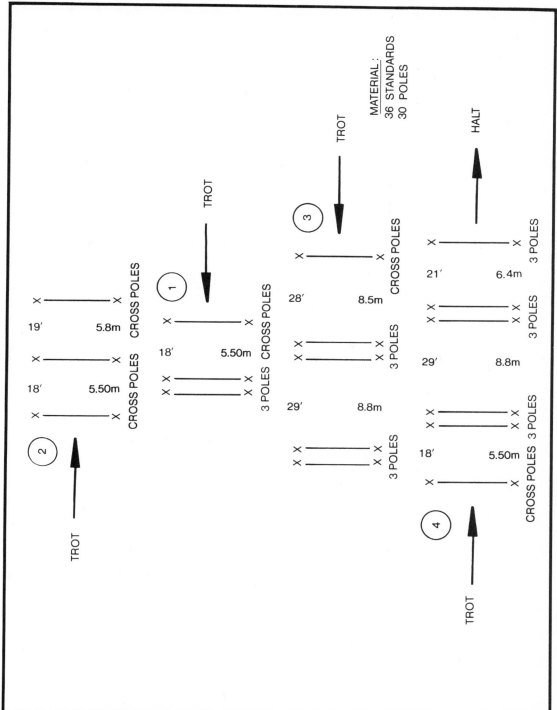

APPENDIX 12

MATERIAL :
36 STANDARDS
30 POLES

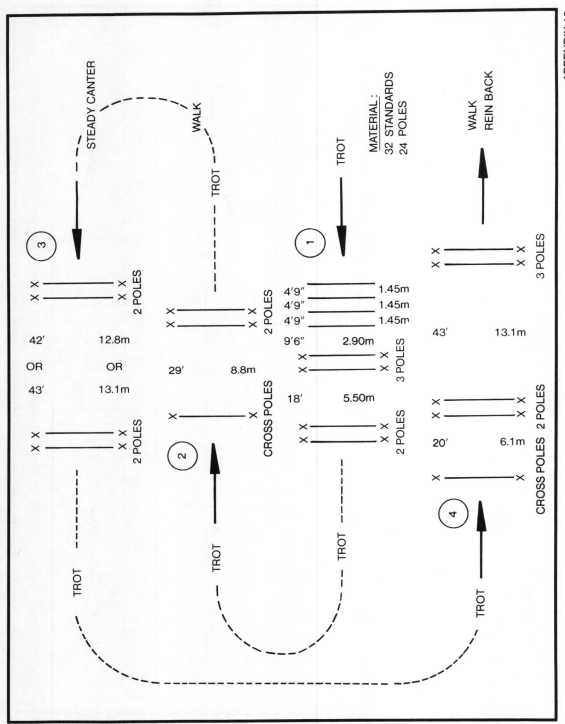

APPENDIX 13

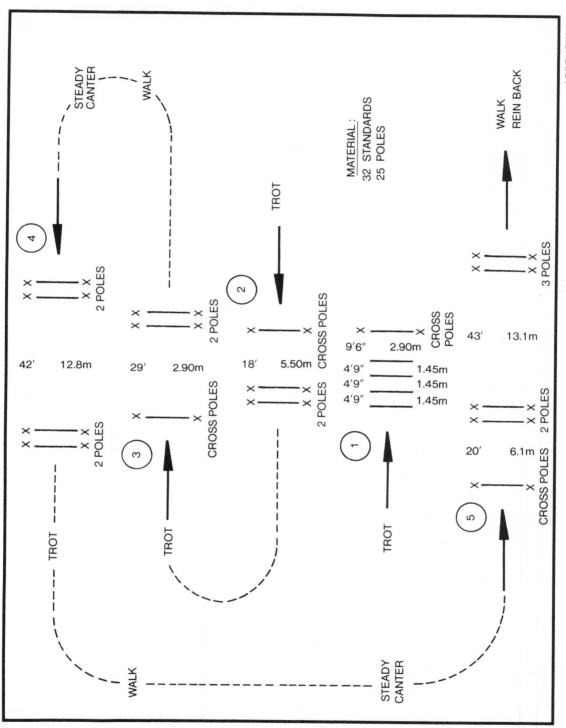

APPENDIX 14

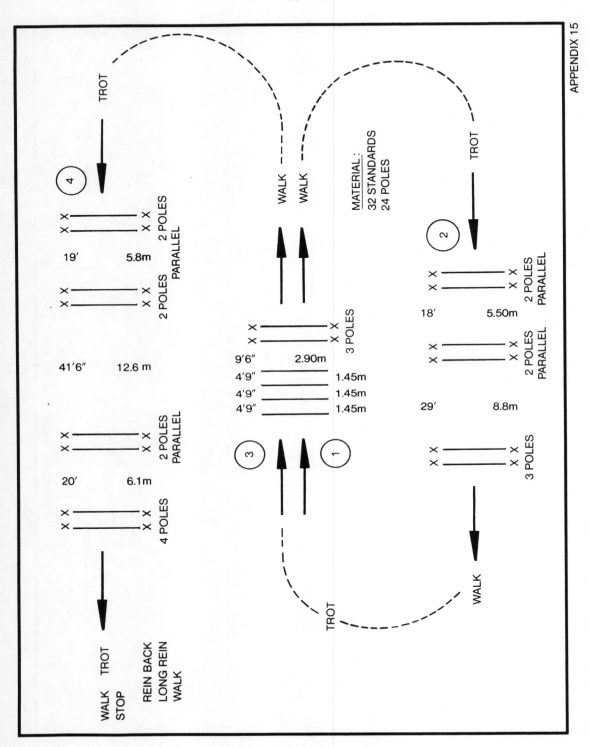

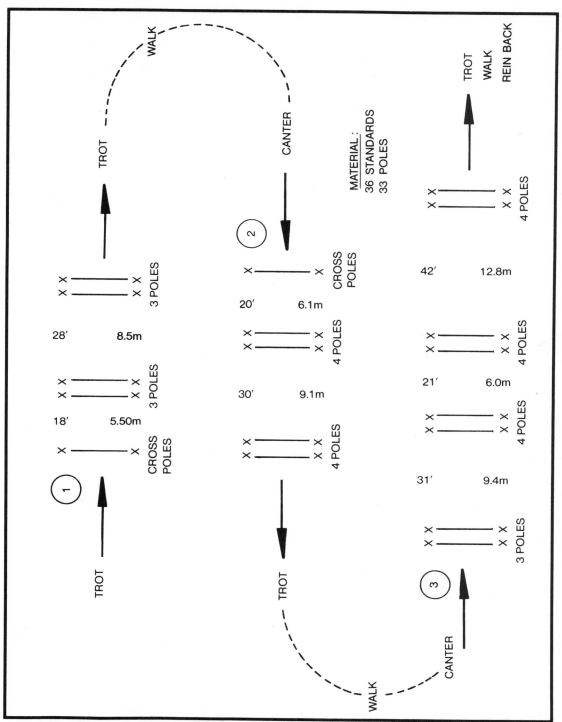

APPENDIX 16

TROT
WALK

CANTER

TROT

CROSS
POLES

20'   6.1m

4 POLES

30'   9.1m

4 POLES

TROT

WALK

CANTER

3 POLES

31'   9.4m

4 POLES

21'   6.0m

4 POLES

42'   12.8m

4 POLES

TROT
WALK
REIN BACK

MATERIAL :
36 STANDARDS
33 POLES

TROT
WALK

3 POLES

28'   8.5m

3 POLES

18'   5.50m

CROSS
POLES

TROT

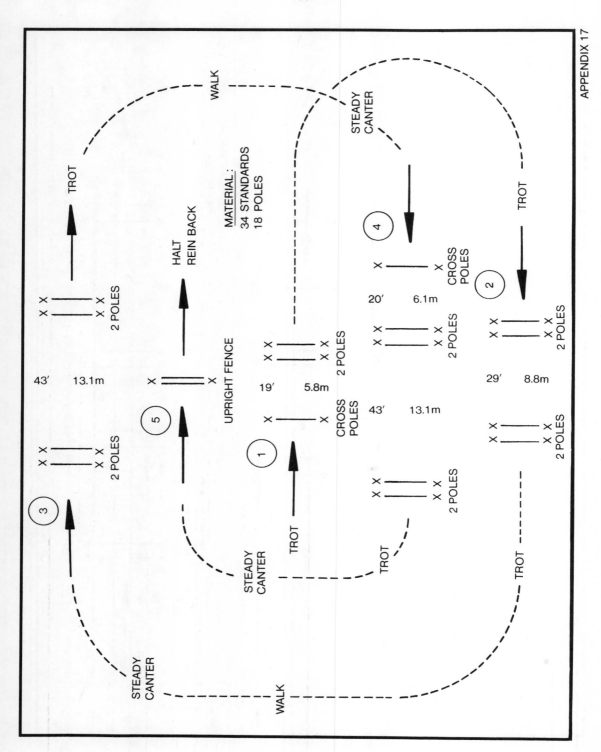

APPENDIX 17

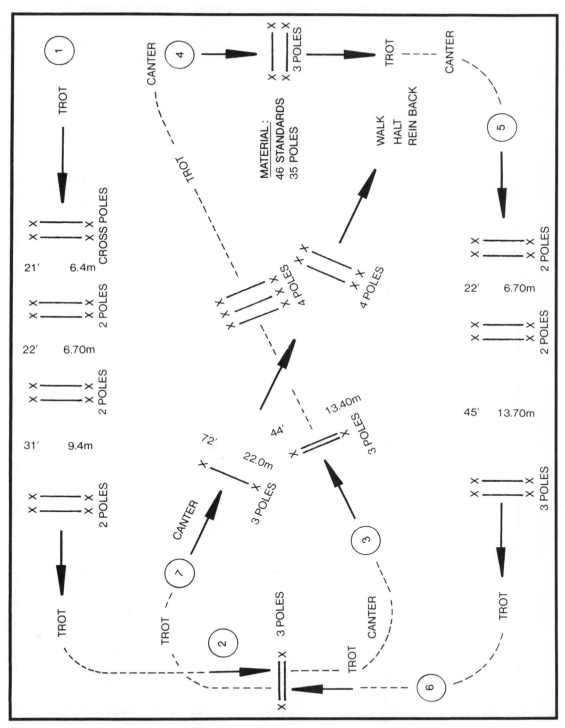

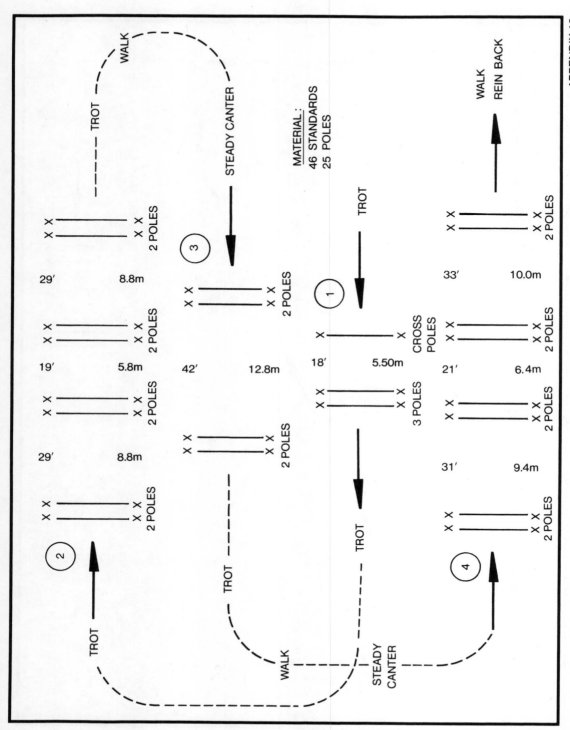

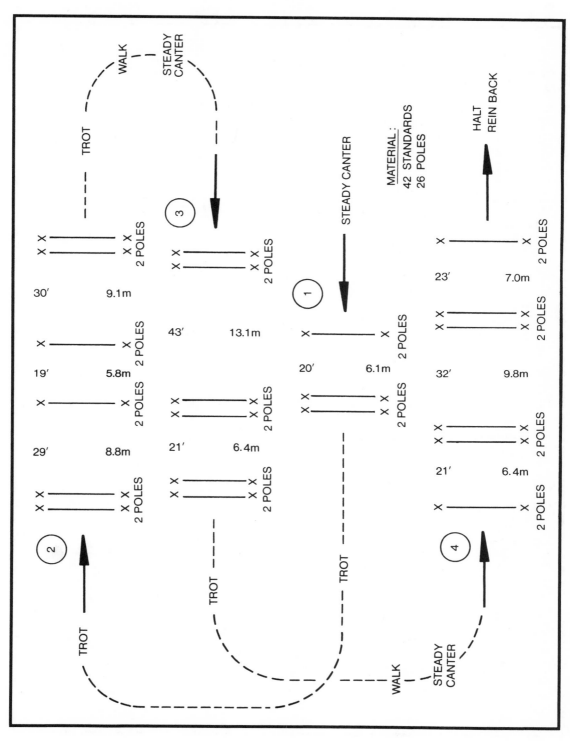

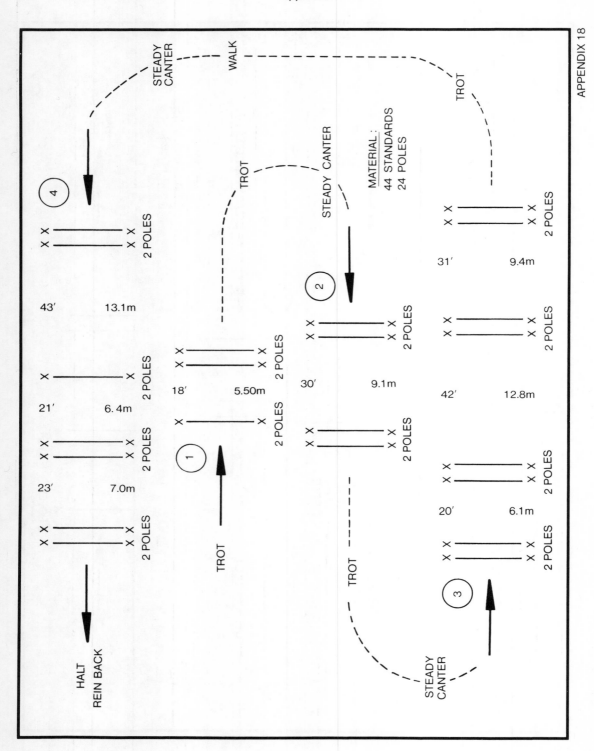

STEADY CANTER

WALK

TROT

MATERIAL :
44 STANDARDS
24 POLES

STEADY CANTER

TROT

STEADY CANTER

④

2 POLES

43'   13.1m

TROT

②

2 POLES

31'   9.4m

2 POLES

2 POLES

X X
X X

2 POLES

18'   5.50m

30'   9.1m

42'   12.8m

×   ×

21'   6.4m

2 POLES

2 POLES

2 POLES

×   ×
×   ×

2 POLES

23'   7.0m

①

2 POLES

2 POLES

20'   6.1m

×   ×
×   ×

2 POLES

2 POLES

×   ×
×   ×

2 POLES

TROT

TROT

③

STEADY CANTER

HALT
REIN BACK

APPENDIX 18

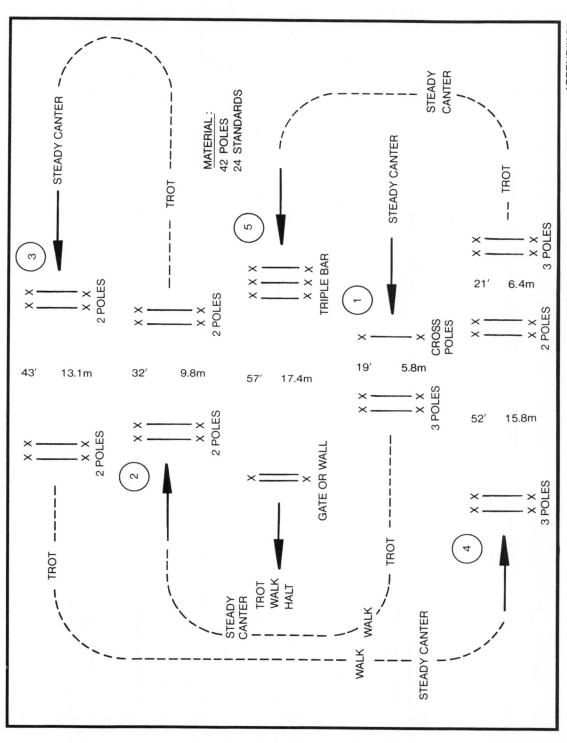

APPENDIX 21

About the Author

BERTALAN DE NÉMETHY was born in Hungary and decided at an early age to become a cavalry officer. After graduating from the Royal Hungarian Military Academy he was appointed to the Royal Military Cavalry School, where he was made an instructor. He also became a member of the Hungarian Olympic Jumping Team, competing throughout Europe. After World War II, he immigrated to the United States, where he was named coach of the U.S. Equestrian Team, a position he held for a quarter century. His teams were victorious in six Olympic Games, five Pan-American Games, and four World Championships. Mr. de Némethy considers his designs for the jumping courses at the second World Cup Finals in Baltimore, Maryland, in 1980, at the Los Angeles Olympiad in 1984, and at the World Cup Finals in Tampa, Florida, in 1989 to have been among his most important achievements. In 1988, Mr. de Némethy produced a series of eight instructional videotapes entitled "The de Némethy Method." He lives with his wife, Emily, in rural New Jersey.

Index